Trinity 101
Father, Son, Holy Spirit

JAMES L. PAPANDREA, PHD

D1547730

Liguori
ONE LIGUORI DRIVE
LIGUORI MO 63057-9999

Imprimi Potest: Harry Grile, CSsR, Provincial
Denver Province, The Redemptorists

Published by Liguori Publications
Liguori, Missouri 63057

To order, visit Liguori.org or call 800-325-9521

Library of Congress Cataloging-in-Publication Data

Papandrea, James Leonard.
 Trinity 101 : Father, Son, and Holy Spirit / James L. Papandrea.—1ˢᵗ ed.
  p. cm.
 1. Trinity. 2. Catholic Church—Doctrines. I. Title. II. Title:
Trinity one hundred one. III. Title: Trinity one hundred and one.
 BT111.3.P37 2012
 231'.044—dc23

                                                                2012013228
 p ISBN 978-0-7648-2082-3
 e ISBN 978-0-7648-6720-0

Compliant with *The Roman Missal*, third edition.

Cover design: Jodi Hendrickson   Cover image: Shutterstock

Liguori Publications, a nonprofit corporation, is an apostolate of The Redemptorists. To learn more about The Redemptorists, visit Redemptorists.com.

Printed in the United States of America
21 20 19 18 17 / 6 5 4 3 2

To my brother, Dr. Rick F. Papandrea

Speed Racer to my Racer X

There are different forms of service but the same Lord.

1 CORINTHIANS 12:5

Contents

Introduction

When I first began studying theology, I did it because I wanted answers to all the deepest questions. However, what one finds when one studies theology is this: Looking into the mysteries of God just reveals deeper mysteries. In my own spiritual life I had to come to a point where I was ready to embrace the mystery. God is a bottomless well, and the understanding of God as Trinity is both the heart of the mystery and the very definition of Christianity (*Catechism of the Catholic Church* 234, hereafter abbreviated *CCC*).

So we approach this task with a lot of humility. This does not mean the task should not be undertaken. Trying to understand the nature of God is not an exercise in futility—it is a worthy exercise—but it is one that should begin and end with the admission that "the foolishness of God is wiser than human wisdom" (1 Corinthians 1:25). In the tradition of Saint Augustine (*faith leads to understanding*) and Saint Anselm (*faith seeking understanding*), we start with what we believe, based on what has been revealed to us in sacred Scripture, and then we try to understand it—not to be master over it, but in a very practical sense to be able to explain our faith to others (1 Peter 3:15).

Another way of saying this is that we admit we could never fully understand the Trinity, because the Trinity is God. If this were not so, believing would not require faith. What we're trying to do here is understand the *doctrine* of the Trinity, or the way that God as Trinity has been revealed to humanity, and understood and explained throughout the history of the Church. My hope is that this book will be part of that process of understanding.

CHAPTER 1

The Trinity in Scripture

What Do We Mean When We Say: "GOD?"

Before we begin, we should clarify something. We say "God" often—many times without giving it much thought—and although we may assume that everyone knows what the word means, we are not always precise or consistent in our use of it. In fact, we actually use the word in several different ways. As Christians, we also say that Jesus Christ is God, but what does that really mean?

Whenever we say "God," we mean one of three things. First, "God" can refer to the Supreme Being in a general sense, and for Christians that means the Trinity. Second, "God" can be used more specifically to mean God the Father, the first person of the Trinity. Third, we may use "God" to mean that which is divine, or divinity itself. When we use it in this way, the word can be as much an adjective as a noun. Technically speaking, Jesus Christ is God, but only if we mean it in the third sense. Jesus is not the Trinity and Jesus is not the first person of the Trinity, the Father. But we do believe that Christ is divine. Most Christians are familiar with the beginning of the Gospel of John: "In the beginning was the Word, and the Word was with God and the Word was God" (John 1:1). This passage could be paraphrased as follows, since this is what it means: "In the beginning was the Son, and the Son was with the Father, and the Son was divine."

As we will see, it is important to be clear that the Son is not the Father and the Son is not the Trinity. Likewise, the Father is not the Son, and the Father is not the Trinity. Therefore, I would advocate for a greater attention to precision of meaning when we as Christians use the term "God." We should not assume that everyone automatically knows what we mean.

THE TRINITY IN THE OLD TESTAMENT

Ultimately, the doctrine of the Trinity comes from Scripture. However it is not spelled out in the apostolic documents as clearly as we might like it to be. In fact, early Christians debated the interpretation of these Scriptures for centuries to come to the understanding of the Trinity that we have now. So when we look at passages that reveal God as Trinity, we do so with the realization that it is not enough just to quote certain Scripture texts. These passages require study that takes into account their biblical and historical context, and they require interpretation within the community of the faithful (2 Peter 1:20). Christian doctrine developed over time, meaning that the Church's understanding increased with the ongoing process of question and debate (*CCC* 65–66). This is the process that took several centuries and many controversies to complete, and it resulted in the Creeds of the Church. Having acknowledged this, let's look at some of the Old Testament passages that Christians have traditionally interpreted as pointing to the Trinity. I encourage you to look these up and read them in context.

Genesis 1:1–2. At the beginning of our Bible, we read the story of creation. We find that even before creation, the Spirit of God hovered over the void in anticipation of creating order out of chaos. The Hebrew word for Spirit can also be translated as "wind," which is why some versions of the Bible describe a "wind from God" (see also Exodus 14:21, 15:8, and John 3:8). The word can also be translated "breath" (for example, see Psalm 33:6, 104:29-30, and John 20:22). However, Christians have historically interpreted this as a reference to the Holy Spirit. It is important to notice here that the Holy Spirit is active in creation, so that it is as appropriate to call the Spirit Creator as it is to call God the Father Creator.

Genesis 1:3-25. Continuing on in the creation story, we read that God (the Father) created the universe by speaking everything into existence. In other words, God creates by his word. Although God does not actually need to speak out loud to create, the point is that creation is the result of the will of God. In Genesis, God's will is externalized by his command, or his word. Christians have traditionally associated this creative speech of God with the title, "Word of God," as it is used of Jesus Christ. John began his gospel with the same words that begin the book of Genesis, "In the beginning..." and then he goes on to refer to Jesus Christ as the Word of God (John 1:1-2, 14). This is not a coincidence. Calling Christ the divine Word of God means that he is the means, or the *agent,* of creation through whom all things were created (John 1:3). This also means that, just like the Holy Spirit, the Word—or Son of God—was active in creation and may also be called Creator.

Genesis 1:26. Notice in this passage that God (the Father) seems to be speaking to someone. Who is the *us* in "Let us make..."? While there are various ways to interpret this, Christians have traditionally understood this passage as though the Father was speaking to the Son, and perhaps also the Spirit. Thus, already in the first chapter of the Bible, these verses have historically been interpreted as pointing to the preexistence of the Son (he existed before he became human, and he was there at creation), the divinity of the Son and Spirit (as "co-Creator" with the Father), as well as the distinction between the Father, Son, and Spirit.

Psalm 51:11-13. In this psalm of confession traditionally attributed to David, the author begs to avoid what would apparently be a punishment for sin: that the Holy Spirit of God might be taken from him. This is one of the first times that the Spirit is called the "Holy Spirit," although the word "holy" here was probably originally meant to be more of an adjective than a title. Nevertheless, this passage seems to be an anticipation of the indwelling of the Spirit as described in 1 Corinthians 6:19, though it also could be understood in terms of the anointing of the Holy Spirit on a king or the inspiration of the Holy Spirit in a prophet. The point is that there is a Holy Spirit who is not identical with God the Father, but who is described as the Holy Spirit of God.

Isaiah 7:14. This is one of many Old Testament passages that the apostles interpreted as a prophecy of the coming of Jesus. In the gospels we are told that *Immanuel* means, "God with us" (Matthew 1:23, see John 1:14). Therefore, the Church has always understood this passage to be about more than the miraculous birth of Christ. It is about the divinity of Christ, that he was the very presence of God on earth. Given this conviction, the Church would come to conclude that it is appropriate to worship him.

Isaiah 9:5-6. These verses may be more familiar to us from Handel's *Messiah* than from the Bible, but that only highlights the fact that this passage is also considered by the Church to be a prophecy of the birth of Christ. Although the original author probably had an earthly prince in mind, it would be hard to overlook the fact that the prophecy includes an affirmation that the Child to be born would be called "mighty God," and even "everlasting Father." We should not press this so far that we think of the Father and the Son as identical (in the original context it only meant that the new king would be a father figure). However, this passage has traditionally been interpreted as pointing to the divinity of Christ (see John 10:30, where Jesus says, "The Father and I are one").

Isaiah 40:13. Here the Holy Spirit is called "the Spirit of the Lord." Although the original audience would not have interpreted this in a Trinitarian sense, the early Christians would have pointed to this verse as evidence of the divine personhood of the Spirit. In this passage, the Spirit of the Lord seems to be more than simply an extension of God or God's attributes. In other cases, such as Zechariah 4:6, the concept of the Spirit of God may be more of a metaphor for the power of God. But even in that case, as an extension of God's power, the Holy Spirit is coming to be described as distinct from God the Father.

Isaiah 61:1. In this passage, quoted by Jesus in Luke 4:16–21, the "Spirit of the Lord God" is the divine inspiration of the prophets. For other examples of the Holy Spirit as the inspiration of the prophets, see also Numbers 11:17, 25–29, 2 Samuel 23:2, Isaiah 11:2–3, Joel 3:1–2 (2:28–29), Zechariah 7:12 and 12:10. These passages have been interpreted by the Church as examples of the existence of the Holy Spirit as both divine and yet distinct from the Father.

Isaiah 63:10–11, 14. In verses ten and eleven, we see the Spirit called God's "Holy Spirit," as in Psalm 51. We can see from verse fourteen that the Holy Spirit is the same as the Spirit of the Lord.

Isaiah 63:16. God (the first person of the Trinity) is referred to by several names in the Old Testament. In fact, scholars often identify different Old Testament authors by the name(s) used for God. It is in Isaiah that God is first referred to as "Father," specifically, "our Father." To the descendants of Abraham, the fatherhood of God meant that he was their provider and protector. Notice that in this passage, the Father is also described as "Redeemer," which reminds us that we should not assume that the Son of God is the only one who can be called Savior.

Isaiah 64:7. Here again, God is called, "our Father." In this context the fatherhood of God refers to God as Creator, and also as the one who forgives the sins of his people. This implies that as Creator, God the Father is also the one who has the right to judge his creation. In the apocryphal book of Third Maccabees, God is the overseer of all things and is called "the first Father of all" (3 Maccabees 2:21, though this line is not in the Septuagint, the Greek Old Testament that was used by Jesus and the apostles).

Daniel 7:13–14. In Daniel's famous vision, he sees "one like a son of man" approaching the "Ancient of Days" in the heavenly realm. Jesus himself made reference to this passage when he called himself "Son of Man," so it should be no surprise that, from the beginning of the Church, Christian theologians have interpreted Daniel's vision as a vision of the preincarnate Christ. The "Ancient of Days" was understood to be God the Father, and the "one like a son of man" was understood to be Christ the Son. In the third century, Saint Hippolytus wrote that Daniel called the Messiah, "one *like* a Son of Man," because he was seeing a vision of Christ before the Incarnation, so before he became a human (Hippolytus, *Against Noetus* 4). The fact that the Father and Son were there together was taken as proof of Christ's preexistence and was connected to John 1:1 and Philippians 2:6. Also, many interpreters would assume that the divinity of Christ is at least implied in this passage. At the same time, the fact that the Son can "approach" the Father implies that they are distinct—the Father and Son are not one and the same.

The Angel of the Lord. This is a phrase that occurs in over fifty Old Testament passages. It was understood by many early Christian theologians as a reference to the preincarnate Christ, the Word of God. In other words, before the human birth of Jesus, he existed eternally in his divine nature and occasionally made an appearance on earth. "Angel," then, was not interpreted as a reference to a created spiritual being, but it was understood according to the literal meaning of the Greek word, *angelos*— that is, a messenger. Therefore, the Word of God was the Father's messenger in the time before the earthly life of Jesus.

A similar and important passage is the visitation of the Lord to Abraham in Genesis chapter 18. There we read that, on one hand, it was the Lord who came to Abraham (verse 1), but on the other hand, Abraham saw "three men" (verse 2). Abraham bowed down to the three men in what seems to be an attitude of worship, and then one of the "three men" promised that he would return the following year when Abraham's wife, Sarah, will have a child. Later (verses 13–14, 22), this "man" is revealed to be the Lord, who again promised to return when Sarah has a child.

However, the Church fathers had read that no one can see God and live (Exodus 33:20–23, John 1:18, see also 1 Timothy 6:16). Yet there were times like these when people apparently saw the divine presence and lived to tell about it. On occasion, a person does seem to see God, who accepts worship and makes promises in the first person, thus ruling out the possibility that it was a mere (created) angel. So the early Church writers reasoned that it was actually God the Father whom no one could see, but God the Son could be seen. Therefore, when it was said that people saw God, they were not seeing God the Father, rather they were seeing a pre-Incarnation manifestation of God the Son. Genesis 18, then, was interpreted by the earliest Christians as another reference to the "Angel of the Lord," the Word of God who visited Abraham accompanied by two regular angels (Genesis 19:1). Later, the "three men" were interpreted as a reference to the Trinity.

In addition to being understood as Old Testament affirmations of the Trinity, these passages are important for what they implied about the distinction between the Father and the Son. One difference between the Father and the Son is that of invisibility versus visibility. In other words, it was assumed that God the Father could never be visible, but God the Son could be visible (see John 1:14, "we saw his glory"). Certainly the Son was visible in his Incarnation, so the Church fathers reasoned that even before the Incarnation, when he came to earth as the Father's messenger, he was able to be temporarily visible and tangible to humanity. There were various explanations for how this was possible, but the point is that even before his human life, the visibility and tangibility of the Son (or at least the possibility of it) is something that distinguished him from the Father.

However, the visibility of the Son is actually evidence of a deeper issue. Christian theologians have always assumed that God is over and above creation, such that God cannot be contained within creation. The theological term for this is *circumscribability*. God cannot be *circumscribed*, or surrounded by anything. However, the obvious fact that the person of Jesus Christ was localized within creation (he was only in one place at a time) might seem to argue against his divinity. To answer this, the early Church fathers reasoned that circumscribability was a personal property of the Son, which distinguished him from the Father, even before the Incarnation. In other words, just as the Son might be visible and tangible, while the Father would not, the Son could also be circumscribed in time and space, while the Father would never be. This is a function of the Son's human nature, however it is not as simple as saying that only the human nature of the Son is circumscribed, since he could manifest himself within time and space even before his Incarnation. At the same time, it must be emphasized that this personal property of the Son does not diminish his divinity or the omnipresence of his divine nature in any way.

THE TRINITY IN THE NEW TESTAMENT

There are various New Testament passages in which the apostles mention the Trinity or bless their readers in the name of the Trinity, all of which demonstrates that these apostles understood God as Father, Son, and Holy Spirit (see for example, 1 Corinthians 12:4–6, 2 Corinthians 13:13, and 1 Peter 1:2). This also demonstrates that even in the earliest years of the Church, the apostles could assume that their readers knew what they meant by Father, Son, and Holy Spirit. In fact, in the early days of the Church, the most pressing question was not about the Trinity in general but about the relationship of Jesus Christ to the God whom he called his Father. In other words, if Christ is divine, what does that mean? Is he identical to the Father? It would seem that cannot be the case, since he talks to the Father and prays to the Father. So what is their relationship, and in what way is Jesus to be thought of as included in the Divine? Questions like these required that the Church sort out its understanding of the person of Christ in order to try to understand the bigger picture of the Trinity.

Therefore, in the New Testament and the early Church, it is not possible to make a clean distinction between christology and Trinitarian theology. Christology, or the study of the person of Christ, is an essential component of the Trinity, and the doctrine of the person of Christ is interdependent with the doctrine of the Trinity. I would argue that there is no real division between Trinitarian theology and christology, since it was the coming of Christ, his life and ministry and his death and resurrection that caused his followers to have to explain him and his relationship to the Father. Christology and the doctrine of the Trinity together are the Church's answer to Jesus' question, "Who do you say that I am?" (Matthew 16:15).

One final word of explanation is in order before we look at the Trinity in the New Testament. Labels such as "high" christology and "low" christology are to be avoided as misleading and counterproductive. For example, it is often taught that the Gospel of John represents a "high" christology because it is thought to emphasize the divinity of Jesus more than his humanity. Not only is this a misinterpretation of the fourth gospel, but if in fact it did emphasize Jesus' divinity over his humanity, then it would be presenting an unbalanced picture of Christ. In other words, a "high" christology that overemphasized Christ's divinity, or a "low" christology that overemphasized Christ's humanity would both be heresy, because each would deny or deemphasize one of Christ's two natures. Orthodox christology is neither "high" nor "low," and thus it is inaccurate to use these labels to describe the christology of the Scriptures. We must always keep in mind that the Scriptures define our doctrine for us. We are not to evaluate them.

What Jesus Said About the Trinity

Jesus as the Son of the Father. In the baptism of Jesus (Matthew 3:13–17, Mark 1:9–11, Luke 3:21–22), the early Christians saw a picture of the Trinity: The Father in the heavenly voice, the Son in the waters of the river Jordan, and the Holy Spirit in the dove. This Holy Spirit is the "Spirit of the Lord" of the Old Testament. The same Spirit who inspired the prophets anoints Jesus (see Acts 10:38). After his baptism and anointing, the heavenly voice of the Father declares that Jesus is his beloved Son. In the transfiguration as well (Matthew 17:1–8, Mark 9:2–8, Luke 9:28–36), the voice of the Father declares that Jesus is his beloved Son, and that all should listen to him.

But what does it mean for God the Father to call Jesus his Son? And what can we glean from the words of Jesus as a clue to his own understanding of his sonship? In a way, we are all sons and daughters of God, and yet there is something unique about the way in which Jesus is the Son of God. This uniqueness will be explained below, but first it is important to see that in the gospels, the sonship of Jesus is described in two different ways. He is called both the Son of God and the Son of Man.

The title "Son of God" carries the cultural assumptions of the heir, the first-born son who exercises his father's authority and stands to inherit all that belongs to the father (see Matthew 21:33–46, Mark 12:1–12, and Luke 20:9–19). Note that in the parable of the wicked tenants, the Son is called "beloved," just as in the baptism and transfiguration of Jesus. Notice also that the question of Luke 10:25 is how one might *inherit* eternal life. Jesus, as the heir of God, is the one who controls the inheritance (see John 1:12). Furthermore, the concept of sonship also has an aspect of apprenticeship to it. As the Son of God, Jesus does the work of the Father.

Jesus rarely used the title Son of God for himself, though he did accept it when others used it of him (Matthew 4:1–11, 14:33, 16:16–17, Mark 3:11, 14:61–62, Luke 22:70). Part of the reason for his avoidance of the term must have been out of Jewish reluctance to say the divine name, as we see in Mark 14:61–62, where the high priest asked him if he was the Son of the "Blessed One" (see also Luke 1:32, 35). Jesus did, however, refer to himself as the Son of the Father (Matthew 11:27/Luke 10:22, Matthew 24:36/Mark 13:32, Matthew 28:19), and his enemies assumed that he had called himself the Son of God (Matthew 27:43). In the Gospel of John, Jesus does use the phrase "Son of God" eight times: John 5:18–23, 25–27, 6:40, 8:36, 10:36–38 (see Matthew 27:43), 11:14, 14:3, 17:1.

There is also a sense in which avoidance of the term could be justified by the potential for misunderstanding in the Greco-Roman world. On the one hand, a son of a god might mean a hero of Greek mythology. On the other hand, the Romans were getting used to the idea of thinking of their emperors as divine. Since a dead emperor would be proclaimed a god by the senate, his (adopted) son and heir—the present emperor—might call himself the son of a god. In the early empire, precisely the time of the early Church, emperors increasingly demanded to be called by divine titles. Therefore, when it is used of Jesus, "Son of God" has a political overtone and a treasonous one at that. Jesus is the Son of God, over against the emperor who is proclaimed a son of a god.

Jesus' preferred title for himself seems to have been "Son of Man." He even used it as a roundabout way to refer to himself when he could have simply said, "me," or "I" (see, for example, Matthew 16:13). When we first encounter the phrase "son of man" in the Old Testament, it simply means a human being. In fact, sometimes it was used to remind someone that he is *only* a human and call to mind his place in relation to God (Job 25:6). But eventually it came to mean the human that God cares for (Psalm 8:4, 144:3) and then a human who is chosen by God (Ezekiel 2:1–3). And thus the term comes to have a connotation that is something like a prophet or even an anointed one. By the time of Daniel, the Messiah is called, "one like a son of man," which many took to mean that he is human, but also more than human (Daniel 7:13–14). He is not a mere human because he comes (originates) from the presence of God, which Christians interpreted as a reference to Christ's preexistence (see John 1:1, Philippians 2:6–7). In reality, the passage in Daniel does not say that the "one like a son of man" comes *from* the Ancient of Days, but the point is that he was in the presence of God before the Incarnation, and he does come "with the clouds of heaven," which could be connected to 1 Thessalonians 4:16–17. In any case, by the time of Jesus, the meaning of the title "Son of Man" had evolved to the point where some Jewish apocalyptic writings included an image of a superhuman Messiah (Sirach 24:1–10, 30–31, 1 Enoch 46:1–8, 48:4–10, 51:3–5, 52:4–9, 61:8–9, 2 Esdras/4 Ezra 13). Therefore, by the time of Jesus' ministry "Son of Man" was a messianic term and implied something more than a mere human. When Jesus called himself the Son of Man, he was making a deliberate connection to Daniel's vision (Daniel 7:13–14). He clearly saw himself as one who comes from the Father to be the savior of humanity (Luke 19:10), the one who will mediate and reconcile humanity to God.

Incidentally, this is why Bible translations that paraphrase "Son of Man" as simply "human being" or "human one" are inadequate. The evolution of meaning in the title is lost, as is the connection of Jesus' self-designation to the Old Testament. The fact that Jesus was intentionally reminding his audience of Daniel chapter 7 every time he called himself Son of Man cannot be overstated.

In the early centuries of the Church, theologians speculated that the title "Son of God" referred to Christ's divinity, while the title "Son of Man" referred to his humanity. However, as Jesus used it, the "Son of Man" does not simply refer to his human nature. It assumes his humanity but implies his divinity as the agent of God. By the third century, the title would again take on the fuller meaning that it had in the gospels, in that it points to both natures. Christ's divine nature is demonstrated by the fact that he is the one who descends from the presence of God to humanity. His human nature is demonstrated by the fact that he is the one who represents humanity to God. As the Son of the Father, Jesus Christ is the Father's heir and anointed representative, representing God to the people, and the people to God.

At the end of Matthew's Gospel, Jesus gives the apostles their mission: to spread the good news, baptize converts and disciple them by teaching them what Jesus taught (Matthew 28:16–20). Within this passage is the Trinitarian baptismal formula; the triune God named as Father, Son, and Holy Spirit (verse 19). Today many scholars maintain that Jesus never actually said these words, that they represent a later development of both liturgy and theology and that they were added to the story when the gospel was written to reflect the current sacramental practice of Matthew's church(es). However, there is no reason to believe that this Trinitarian formula could not have originated with Jesus. No one denies that Jesus called God "Father" and taught his disciples to do the same. Jesus also taught his disciples about the Holy Spirit (Matthew 12:32, Mark 13:11, Luke 11:13, John 14:26, 15:26). Finally, though Jesus apparently did not prefer to call himself the Son of God, Matthew 28:19 does not say "Son *of God*," so that there is no reason to believe that Jesus could not have referred to himself as the Son and understood himself to be in a relationship with the Father and the Spirit that would be expressed in this way. Even if it could be demonstrated beyond a doubt that Jesus never spoke these words or taught the Trinitarian formula, the presence of it in the Gospel of Matthew at least proves that it was in use by the middle of the first century, for even if it were added by the evangelist, it was certainly not new at that time. That being the case, there are at most only a few decades from Jesus to the time we know the formula to be in use. This begs the question whether it is more likely that it comes from Jesus, or that something Jesus never taught gained such acceptance in so short a time. Therefore I assume that the Trinitarian formula of Father, Son, and Holy Spirit does indeed originate with Jesus.

In the Great Commission, then, Jesus clarifies not only the mission of his apostles, but he also teaches them how they should understand him and his relationship to God. He has referred to himself as the Son of the Father, and his sonship is expressed in a formula that identifies him with the Divine. His resurrection also shed some light on his relationship to the Father, and with that in mind the apostles were willing to worship him. He sums it up in the very words he used to preface the Great Commission: "All authority in heaven and on earth has been given to me..." (Matthew 28:18). As the possessor of divine authority, he is the heir of the Father. He is the agent and messenger of the Father (Matthew 21:37), yet it is clear that he is not identical with the Father. Therefore, the sonship of Jesus points to his unique relationship with the Father, and yet it also clarifies that Jesus is not simply an Incarnation of the Father.

Jesus as the I AM. Jesus also made certain self-revelatory statements in the Gospel of John that connect him to the God who is revealed in the Old Testament. John 8:58 is interpreted as an indication of Christ's own understanding of his preexistence: "Before Abraham came to be, I am." However, what is equally striking is the way he has intentionally chosen his words to remind his audience of the Father's self-revelation in the burning bush, "I am who I am"—tell them I AM sent you (Exodus 3:14). The fact that those who heard Jesus call himself "I AM" wanted to stone him to death shows that they understood that Jesus was making a radical claim of a unique relationship of equality with the Father (John 8:59, see John 18:6). Thus he claimed to be more than a prophet, more than an anointed man, closer to God than any other human being ever, with the unique authority to speak *for* God and *as* God (John 8:24–28, 13:19, see John 14:6).

Jesus continued this trend in the so-called "I am…" statements, in which he implies that he is the embodiment of Old Testament manifestations of God and a more complete revelation of God than anything seen in the Old Testament. He referred to himself as the Bread of Life that came down from heaven (John 6:26–51, see Exodus 16:4). Not only does this connect Jesus with God's revelation in the Old Testament through the "I am…" saying, it also implies his preexistence and his divinity in the concept of descent from heaven (see Daniel 7:13, Philippians 2:7). In the same way, he also referred to himself as the Light of the World (John 1:8, 8:12, 9:5, see Genesis 1:3), the Door to safety for the sheep (John 10:1–10, see Isaiah 53:6), the Good Shepherd (John 10:11–16, see Ezekiel 34:2–31), the True Vine (John 15:1–5, see Isaiah 5:7) and the Way, the Truth and the Life (John 11:25, 14:6, see Psalm 25:5).

As the presence of divinity on earth, the person of Jesus replaced the Temple (Matthew 26:61, see John 2:18–22). When Jesus cleansed the Temple, he showed he had authority over it, but more than that, Jesus himself became the focus of worship for Christians, especially after the destruction of the Temple in 70. The continuing presence of Christ, even after the resurrection and ascension, was considered a divine presence (Matthew 18:20, see 28:20). The statement of Jesus in Matthew 18:20 seems to be based on a rabbinic saying, "If two sit together and the words of the law are spoken between them, the Divine Presence rests between them." Clearly by stating it in the way he does, Jesus has equated himself with the Divine Presence. All this contributes to the early Christians' belief in the divinity of Christ and the conviction that it is appropriate to worship him.

The worship of Jesus in the gospels begins with the adoration of Mary's newborn by the Magi (Matthew 2:11). Later, when Jesus walked on water, his disciples responded by worshiping him (Matthew 14:22–33). Finally, after the resurrection, Jesus' followers were apparently even more willing to worship him, though even then some doubted (Matthew 28:9, 17). While it is true that the worship of Jesus during his life was tentative at best, there was never a time when the Church did not worship him, and the early Church certainly understood its liturgical worship of Christ to be consistent with the reverence shown to him by the Magi, the shepherds, and the apostles. In the minds of the earliest Christians, the worship of Jesus was considered to be consistent with what he taught about himself and therefore was not a form of idolatry. Worship of Jesus was connected to the belief in him as the unique Son of the Father (Matthew 14:33), and by accepting the Son, one was really accepting the Father who sent him (Mark 9:37). To worship Jesus was to worship the presence of God, and to fail to worship Jesus would have been seen as rejecting the Father by rejecting the Son whom he sent (Luke 10:16).

Jesus on the Holy Spirit. All four gospels and the book of Acts tell us that Jesus would baptize his followers with the Holy Spirit (Matthew 3:11, Mark 1:8, Luke 3:16, John 1:33, Acts 1:5). Later we find out that this baptism with the Holy Spirit is the same as the giving of the gift of the Holy Spirit to believers (Acts 11:15–16). The same Spirit of God who inspired the prophets and apostles would be given by Christ to his Church (Luke 11:13, John 20:22). Jesus promised that the Father would send the Holy Spirit in his name (John 14:26). Or to put it another way, he promised that he would send the Holy Spirit from the Father (John 15:26). This indicates that the Father is the primary and ultimate Source of the Spirit, and yet as the Father's agent it can be said that the Spirit also comes from the Son, because the Son gives the Spirit to the Church. As the theologians would later say, the Spirit comes *from* the Father *through* the Son.

In the Gospel of John, Jesus refers to the Holy Spirit as the Spirit of Truth and the Advocate (John 14:15–17, 14:26, 15:26, 16:13, *CCC* 2625). This latter term is a translation of the Greek word *paraclete,* which in other versions of the Bible is sometimes translated "Helper," "Comforter," "Counselor," or even "Companion." Notice that Jesus called the Spirit, "*another* Advocate*,*" indicating that Jesus himself is also properly described as our Advocate. However, after his ascension, he gave the Holy Spirit to the Church to stay with us, and "guide [us] to all truth" (John 16:13–15). This includes a promise that the apostles would be inspired to write the documents of the New Testament (John 14:26). Jesus said that the Holy Spirit would convict the world of sin and teach the world about justice (John 16:8–11).

Jesus also promised that those who were arrested for spreading the faith would be inspired by the Holy Spirit to witness to their accusers (Matthew 10:20, Mark 13:11, Luke 12:12). Jesus himself was guided and inspired by the Holy Spirit (Luke 4:1, 4:18–21, 10:21, Acts 1:2). In fact, he admitted that his power came from the Holy Spirit (Matthew 12:28). As some early theologians believed, this is because Jesus had set aside his prerogative to use his own divine power in order truly to experience the weakness of the human condition (Philippians 2:7). This is why Jesus said that his apostles would be able to do even greater things than he did (John 14:12), because they would be given the same Holy Spirit who empowered him (John 7:38–39).

Summary of What Jesus Said About the Trinity. Jesus himself taught his followers how they should "call on the name of the LORD" (Psalm 116). The sacraments of the Church would be conducted in the name of the Father, Son, and Holy Spirit (Matthew 18:19). The God of the Old Testament would now be called "Father," and Jesus claimed a unique relationship to the Father as his Son. This unity of Father and Son was demonstrated by the fact that those who accepted the Son were also accepting the Father (Mark 9:37) and those who rejected the Son were also rejecting the Father (Luke 10:16). The Son is both the apprentice and the agent of the Father, doing the Father's work and coming with the Father's authority (see Matthew 17:5, "Listen to him"). The emperor may claim to be a son of a god, but Jesus Christ is *the* Son of *the* God and the heir to the eternal kingdom. As the Son of Man, Jesus comes from the divine realm to reconcile humanity to the Divine (Daniel 7:13–14). In his divine nature he descends from the Father to reveal the Father to humanity (Matthew 11:27, see John 1:14, 18). In his human nature, he is a descendant of humanity and represents humanity to the Father. Together the Father and the Son grant the gift of the advocacy of the Holy Spirit.

What Paul Said About the Trinity

The Apostle Paul was one of the first to write Christian theology. In fact, the earliest existing Christian documents are the letters of Paul in the New Testament (most of them were written before the gospels). However, it is generally recognized that at times Paul is quoting material that comes from even earlier than the letter he is writing. Sometimes, to support his arguments, Paul used preexisting tradition that his readers would recognize. In other words, there was already a body of tradition in the Church from the first decades following the death and resurrection of Jesus that, to some extent, was recognized in the Pauline churches, and presumably accepted by them. This material is important for several reasons, not the least of which is its proximity to Jesus and the apostles. The fact that this material comes from a time when those who knew Jesus were still alive makes its content extremely valuable as representative of apostolic teaching and earliest tradition. Also, since Paul quotes this material in order to support his own arguments in the letters, we can assume that both he and his audience accept the content of the material as authoritative, otherwise quoting it would risk the rejection of his point.

There are two main types of pre-Pauline material that we can see in Paul's letters. The first type is a collection of fragments of affirmations of faith that were already in use in the Church when Paul was writing his letters. These affirmations were meant to be short summaries of the gospel message itself. Of course, Paul maintained that he is an apostle sent by Christ himself and did not need the sanction of the other apostles for his ministry (Galatians 1:1, 11–17). On the other hand, Paul did also admit that he consulted the other apostles, and it is safe to assume (and does not diminish Paul's apostleship at all) that he received the oral tradition of the details of the gospel message from the other apostles (Galatians 1:18–24, 1 Corinthians 11:2, 15:3). It is also certainly the case that Paul learned some of his theology from early Christian liturgy, especially the sacramental rituals of baptism and the Eucharist. Therefore, this preexisting tradition comes through in Paul's letters, in quotations from early presentations of the gospel message, and in fragments of liturgical statements of faith. The second type of pre-Pauline material also comes from the early liturgical tradition and includes fragments of some of the first Christian hymns. For this second type, we will focus on what appear to be two songs, as examples of some of the earliest expressions of Trinitarian theology.

Affirmations of Faith. In 1 Corinthians 15:1–11, Paul outlines the basic Christian gospel message, which he had received and passed on to his converts. In a nutshell, the gospel message is this: Jesus Christ died, was buried, was raised on the third day and appeared to his disciples, as well as many more people, and all this was a fulfillment of Scripture. If one compares this to Peter's sermon in Acts 2:14–36, the details are the same, as one would expect. However, the most important part is what Peter's version only implies and Paul's makes clear: that Jesus died *for our sins*. In other words, his death has an atoning significance— it makes our forgiveness and reconciliation with God possible. Since it was assumed that only God could forgive sins, this means that the life, death, and resurrection of Jesus was an act of God, which is evidence of the close and unique connection of the Son with the Father. The fact that Paul explicitly states that he is handing on what he received demonstrates that this aspect of the early preaching was not something Paul created but was in fact part of the gospel message before the time of Paul.

There are also fragments of affirmations of faith in Paul's letters that were probably used in liturgy, especially in connection with baptism. When a convert to Christianity was to be baptized, he or she was expected to make a profession of faith. Depending on the time and place, these professions of faith could be as simple as saying, "Jesus is Lord" (1 Corinthians 12:3) or as elaborate as Creeds recited in question-and-answer form ("Do you believe...?"). Since we are usually dealing with excerpts from these statements of faith, it is difficult to say with any certainty what the overall format may have been. However, there are several passages in Paul's letters that point to preexisting material used in this way.

Romans 10:9–10 may be an affirmation of faith, or least the indirect description of one. In fact, some early Christians connected this passage to the liturgy by interpreting the "believing in your heart" as a reference to the hearing of the gospel and the "confessing with your mouth" as a reference to the reciting of the Creed. In this passage, it is Jesus' resurrection that witnesses to his divine nature and justifies the use of the title "Lord." We will explore the title Lord as it was used of Jesus below, but for now note that it is belief in (acceptance of) his lordship and his resurrection that leads to salvation. In the material from 1 Corinthians that we examined above we noted that Jesus' death was directly related to the forgiveness of sins. Now we see that his resurrection is related to salvation. Therefore, it is safe to say that one without the other would not be sufficient. It is Jesus' death and resurrection that make salvation possible. In the early Church, these two aspects of Jesus' ministry were understood to be dramatically reenacted in baptism. A new convert would identify with Jesus' death by going under the water. In coming up from the water, the baptism becomes a proclamation of the promise that those who identify with Christ in this way, though they will die as he died, they will also be raised as he was raised (Romans 8:11). Of course as Jesus instructed, baptism was always conducted in the name of the Trinity: the Father, Son, and Holy Spirit, whom the early theologian Irenaeus called, "the three articles of the seal (of baptism)" (Irenaeus of Lyons, *Demonstration of the Apostolic Preaching* 100, see Ephesians 1:13–14).

Finally, in 1 Corinthians 8:6 we have the closest thing in the New Testament to an actual creed. It does not yet have a Trinitarian formula, since the Holy Spirit is not specifically mentioned, but it does seem to have a creedal format. This statement of faith is as follows (my own translation from the Greek):

> **There is one God, the Father**
> **From whom all things come**
> **And we will return to him**
> **And one Lord, Jesus Christ**
> **Through whom all things come**
> **And we will return through him**

The Greek text has no verbs, so the verbs must be supplied. While many translators supply the verb "to be" (exist, come into being), I have chosen to supply verbs that suggest not only existence, but also direction, to convey that the Father, as Alpha and Omega, is both the Source and destiny of all things. Note that "Alpha and Omega" originally referred to God the Father as the origin and culmination of all existence (Isaiah 41:4, 44:6). With the coming of Christ, however, the Son is now seen as both the agent of creation (John 1:3) and the agent of reconciliation. In John's Revelation, "the Alpha and the Omega" is both the Father (Revelation 1:8, 21:5–6) and the Son (Revelation 22:12–13). This is a clear indication of Christ's divinity, if not also his equality with the Father (see Philippians 2:6). Christ is both the mediator of creation and the mediator of redemption (see Colossians 1:15–20, below).

First Corinthians 8:6 seems to be an expansion of the "creed" of Judaism, the *Shema* (Deuteronomy 6:4). It begins with an affirmation that there is only one God, but then includes Jesus as the one Lord. What the lordship of Christ meant to Paul will be explored below, however at the pre-Pauline stage all we can say with any certainty is that at least it seems to be an attempt to acknowledge the divinity of Christ while reserving the title "God" for the Father. Notice that the one God of the Old Testament is specifically identified as the Father, and yet the designation of Jesus as Lord cannot be taken to imply that there are two Gods. In order to maintain the oneness of God, and yet include Jesus Christ within the Divine, Christ has been inserted into the oneness of God as the mediator (or agent) of both creation and redemption. The Church's conviction that the worship of Christ as divine does not diminish the oneness of God had to be clarified in a way that could be explained to scoffers and taught to the new converts. This "creed" not only affirms the oneness of God as well as the divinity of Christ, it goes even further to say that Christ is the one *through whom* God the Father accomplished the creation of the universe and will accomplish the redemption of creation. We will explore the significance of Christ's role as mediator below, but for now we can say that the agency of Christ in both creation and redemption effectively puts Christ in the divine realm without making him a competitor of the one God. Rather, the common mission of both Father and Son serve to emphasize their unity.

Therefore, as we have already seen, it is just as appropriate to say that the Son of God is Creator as it is to say that the Father is Creator. It is also equally appropriate to say that the Father and the Son are Redeemer. As this way of thinking develops it will eventually come to be named as the doctrine of *inseparable operation.* This is the conviction that all three persons of the Trinity are always unified in all divine activity (*CCC* 258, 267). There is no activity that separates or distinguishes the three persons of the Trinity.

At the same time, however, this early creed does make a distinction between the Father and the Son. The Father is the one *from whom* everything ultimately comes and *to whom* everything ultimately returns. Therefore the Father is, to use a philosophical term, the First Cause of all existence. If one imagines all of creation as the product of a series of cause and effect, the beginning of that series is God—the one who began the "chain reaction" of cause and effect, but who is not the effect (or result) of some prior cause. God is the uncaused cause of all existence. However, the early theologians would clarify that it is technically only God the Father who is the First Cause. God the Son and God the Spirit can be equally called the cause of all creation (that is, the Creator), but the Son and the Spirit are not without a cause—each is dependent on the Father as the Source of even their very existence. The existence of the Son and Spirit is contingent upon the existence of the Father.

However the existence of the Father is neither dependent nor contingent on the Son or the Spirit. The Father is the ultimate Source of all things, while the Son is the Father's agent—still equally involved in creation—but he is not the primary Source. This distinction between the Father and Son will become increasingly important to guard against a confusion of the two (the Son is not the Father), yet the unity of action will support the conviction that although the Son is not the Father, yet there is still only one God. First Corinthians 8:6 attempts to explain this paradox through the language of Source (*from whom*) versus agency (*through whom*).

So far we can see from these pre-Pauline fragments that the earliest Christians understood Jesus Christ to be both divine and human. The divinity of Christ is stated tentatively at this point in deference to the oneness of God and the reservation of the term "God" for the Father, and yet the seeds of a "two natures" christology are planted at the earliest stage in the Church's life. The first Christians believed that his death and resurrection had an atoning significance that made forgiveness and reconciliation with God possible. Finally, they understood the relationship between the Father and the Son to have something of a unity and something of a distinction. The unity is in the common creative and redemptive activity of Father and Son, while the distinction between them is that the Father alone is the First Cause and ultimate Source of all existence.

Early Christian Hymns. The first Christians believed that in Jesus, the promised Messiah had finally come, and this was cause for celebration. Therefore, there was never a time in the Church when Christ was not worshiped. The hymns that the early Christians sang are in fact the earliest written theology, since the worship of Christ came before the need to explain or justify it. In fact, in some ways the practice of worshiping

Christ led to a more clarified explanation of theology as the Christians were forced to justify their belief that Jesus is divine, as well as their conviction that worshiping him was not a form of idolatry. In other words, the practice of worshiping Christ was assumed from the beginning, but only after the practice was established did the Christians face the need to justify it to their Jewish relatives and neighbors. In any case, these early Christian hymns give us some of the first christological statements from the earliest decades of the church. They are the first attempts at expanding the understanding of the Divine to include the person of Christ.

No doubt some hymns were written and offered that did not reflect the person of Christ as the majority of first-generation Christians understood him, but those hymns would eventually have been rejected by the Church at large. However, it is safe to assume that the hymns that Paul quotes had already stood the test of time and scrutiny and had gained acceptance in the Church precisely because they conformed to the apostles' teachings about Christ.

Scholars identify a hymn text within Paul's letters by noting a change in the phrasing of a passage, such that there appears to be a poetic form, with rhythm, repetitions and alliterations. Sometimes the poetry takes the form of parallel couplets or has some other structural symmetry. In addition, there is often an introductory phrase that marks a passage as a quotation. Within the quotation there may be extraneous material not directly relevant to the point Paul is trying to make, as well as words that Paul doesn't normally use. While this evidence in itself does not prove that a passage was a hymn, it seems that the way Paul quotes these passages assumes his audience was familiar with them and implies that these are more than just quotations of Church teaching, they are quotations of memorized, or memorable, material. Paul seems to count on a universal familiarity with these hymns, at least in the cities to which he writes, and he assumes that his audience will accept the content of the hymns (or he would never quote them to support his arguments). In other words, Paul knows what hymns the believers are singing in the churches he has visited. It is interesting to note that his letter to the Christians in Rome, a city which he had not yet visited, does not contain any quotations of hymns.

Although there are several passages in Paul's letters that are often identified as hymn texts, we are going to look at two of them as examples of the way the pre-Pauline tradition described the Trinity. They are Colossians 1:15–20 and Philippians 2:6–11. For each one, I have isolated the lines of poetry (the "lyrics" of the song) and put them into stanzas. This requires making some decisions about what words and phrases may have been added by Paul, which were not in the original hymn. This is done by observing which parts of the text seem to be a departure from the point of the hymn, or do not seem to fit the meter of the poetry. These segments are then assumed to have been added by Paul for emphasis and to bring the audience back to his own point. For my reconstruction of the hymn texts I am indebted to the work of E. Norden, Ralph P. Martin, J.T. Sanders, and F.F. Bruce. The translations from Greek are my own.

Colossians 1:15–20

First stanza:

Christ is the agent of creation	Christ's Preexistence
He is the image of the invisible God	Christ's divinity
The one who brings forth all of creation	Agent of creation
For all things were created by him	All things begin in him
All things have been created through him and for him	He is the center of all
He is before all things	Preexistence
And all things are brought together in him	Mediator of reconciliation

Second stanza:

Christ is the agent of redemption	Christ's Incarnation
He is the source	Christ's divinity
First to come forth from the dead	Agent of redemption
So that in all things he might be the ultimate one	All things end in him
For it seemed good for all the fullness to reside in him	He encompasses all
And through him to reconcile all things to himself	Eschatology
Having made peace through him	Mediator of reconciliation

This quotation in Paul's Letter to the Colossians appears to be a two-stanza hymn, in which Christ is praised as the agent of creation (first stanza) and the agent of redemption (second stanza). The first thing that must be pointed out is the translation of the Greek word that is usually rendered into English as, "firstborn," as in the phrases "firstborn of all creation" and "firstborn from the dead." I have chosen to translate it in the sense of "first to bring forth" to highlight its active sense. Therefore I have rendered the two phrases, "the one who brings forth," and "first to come forth." Once we translate the text in this way, we can see that the first stanza is about Christ as Creator ("the one who brings forth all of creation") and the second stanza is about Christ as Redeemer, by his resurrection ("first to come forth from the dead"). This dual role of Christ as agent of creation and agent of redemption is similar to what we have already seen in 1 Corinthians 8:6.

In the first stanza of the hymn, Christ is the agent, or mediator, of creation. This is explicit in the assertion that all things have come into existence through him (as we also read in John 1:3). This implies the divinity of Christ based on the assumption that only God (the Divine) can be Creator. Not only does this imply his divinity, it also presupposes his preexistence ("he is before all things"). He existed before the creation of the universe, and so also before his Incarnation. The fact that the Son is co-Creator with the Father points to a creative unity between the Father and the Son, yet like 1 Corinthians 8:6, there is also a distinction between the Father and Son implied here. As the Father's agent, the Son is not the Father, but is in fact both co-Creator as well as mediator of Creator and creation. Another distinction found in this hymn is that Christ is "the image of the invisible God." In other words, though God the Father cannot be seen (John 1:18), the Son can be seen and is the visible image of the invisible Father.

In the second stanza, Christ is the agent of redemption. The one through whom the universe was created is the same one through whom creation will be redeemed. Because of this, it is also appropriate to say that he is the beginning and the end (Revelation 21:6, 22:13). In this hymn, redemption is described in terms of reconciliation, or peace. It is assumed that reconciliation is ultimately with the Father, but it is accomplished through the mediation of the Son, just as creation itself was accomplished through the mediation of the Son. Not surprisingly, redemption or reconciliation is directly connected to the resurrection of Christ, the fact that he is the "first to come forth from the dead." His death and resurrection make our resurrection and eternal life possible. He is the pioneer of resurrection because those who follow him in life will follow him in eternal life (Romans 8:11, John 14:1–6).

The second stanza also hints at Christ's divinity when it says that he encompasses "all the fullness." Though the hymn does not elaborate (fullness of what?), Paul expands on this in chapter two, verse nine, where he clarifies that it is the fullness of divinity that resides within him. Notice also that the two stanzas of this hymn correspond to two "phases" in the life of Christ: first, his preexistence, in which he is the agent of creation; second, his Incarnation, in which he is the agent of redemption. In his preexistence, he is fully divine but not yet human. In his Incarnation, he acquires a full humanity while remaining fully divine.

Philippians 2:6–11

First stanza:

Christ is exalted	Preexistence
He existed in the form of God	Preexisting divinity
He did not consider equality with God something to cling to	Divinity
But he emptied himself	Voluntary descent
Taking the form of a servant	Submission

Second stanza:

Christ is humbled	Incarnation
He came to be in the likeness of humanity	Acquired humanity
He was recognized as a man by his appearance	Humanity
He humbled himself	Voluntary descent
Becoming submissive (even to the point of death)	Submission

Third stanza:

Christ is exalted	Exaltation
And therefore God exalted him to the highest	Restored equality
And gave him the name above every name	Divinity
So that at the name of Jesus every knee would bend	We "descend"
And every tongue admit that Jesus Christ is Lord	We submit

This is undoubtedly the most famous of the New Testament hymns. Here we have a three-stanza hymn that expands on the two stanzas of Colossians 1, adding a third phase in the life of Christ, that of his post-ascension exaltation. The most important feature of this passage is the fact that the Incarnation of Christ is described as an "emptying" (in Greek: *kenosis*). The emptying allows the divine and preexistent Word to become human so that he can experience true humanity.

Like the hymn in Colossians, the first phase of the life of Christ is his preexistence, before the Incarnation. In this phase he exists in an exalted state equal to God the Father, and therefore he had to "empty himself" in order to become human. This being the case, it is clear that he started out as more than human before his Incarnation. Therefore, the Church has traditionally interpreted the preexistence, the equality with the Father, and the emptying of Christ in the Incarnation, all as evidence of his divinity. Furthermore, we are told that he existed in the form of God. This goes farther than anything we have seen so far in affirming Christ's divine nature. The early theologians all equated form with nature, so the phrase, "form of God" was interpreted to mean that Christ was always of the same divine nature as the Father. Another way to clarify the terms in these hymns is to think of it like this: being in the *form* of God describes the Son's unity and equality with the Father, while being the *image* of God describes his distinction from the Father (that he is not the Father, because he is the visible *image* of the Father).

I have translated the second line in the first stanza, "he did not consider equality with God something to cling to." In some versions of the Bible, this line is translated using terms like, "grasp." While the sense of the Greek could be rendered this way, the context requires that we understand this, not as something that would be "taken," or "stolen," but as something that would be "kept" or "held on to." The important point is that equality with the Father is something Christ always had— it was not something that he lacked and might have coveted or tried to acquire. We have here the first hint of something that will be important later, for while there are multiple texts in the Scriptures that witness to Christ's preexistence, here the explicit claim of equality with God implies that his existence is eternal. In other words, even John 1:1, which says that the

Word preexisted creation, still leaves open the possibility that he could have had a beginning to his existence prior to creation (we will see why this is important later). However, here in Philippians 2:6, we have the hint that Christ is not only preexistent, he is *eternally* preexistent, just as the Father is, because in his divine nature (the form of God), he is equal to the Father.

In verse 7, we see that Christ was willing to set aside the glory and the prerogatives of his equality with the Father and "empty" himself in order to become human and accept the humility of the human condition. This does not imply that Christ ceased to be in the form of God or that he emptied himself of divinity in the Incarnation. It is very important to keep in mind that Christ did not cease to be divine in his Incarnation and earthly life, nor did he become any less divine. The emptying, or *kenosis*, was not a change in the divine nature of Christ, and he did not cease to be of equal divinity with the Father. It can be thought of as more of a sending, a "descent" from the divine realm to the world of humanity, in which he acquired a human nature and accepted the limitations of human existence. This descent is the Incarnation, when the divine Word became flesh. During his life on earth he voluntarily and temporarily chose not to exercise divine power, since it would be impossible to experience true humanity (and the human condition) while taking advantage of omnipotence or omnipresence.

Furthermore, Christ didn't just become human, he became a servant. Some Bibles translate this word as "slave," and while that is a faithful translation of the Greek, I've chosen to use the word "servant" to emphasize that his servanthood was voluntary. The Son's equality with the Father requires that any submission or humiliation must be voluntary, since the Divine cannot be forced to do anything against his will. It is interesting to note that while Philippians 2:7 is based on Isaiah 53:12, it is not based on the Septuagint, the Greek Old Testament most in use at the time of the apostles. The Greek of Philippians 2:7 is based on the Hebrew version of Isaiah. The difference is that the Septuagint says, "his soul was delivered to death" (passive), while the Hebrew text says, "he poured out his life to the point of death" (active). Apparently, the Hebrew text was chosen precisely because it emphasizes that Christ's death was a *voluntary* sacrifice. He emptied himself, no one emptied him. He accepted the form of a servant, no one forced it on him.

Thus the second stanza of this hymn focuses on Jesus' Incarnation, which is his human life and ministry, his humiliation and suffering and his death. Here again we see the two natures of Christ affirmed, he has always existed in the form of God, and he took on the form of humanity—true divinity and true humanity.

The third stanza reveals that after his death and resurrection, Christ was restored to his prior place of glory, acknowledging his equality with the Father (see Isaiah 45:23). He has been to the lowest place of humility, suffering, and death, then he was exalted to the highest status in the heavenly realm. While the resurrection is not specifically mentioned, it is assumed as the vindication of his innocence. His ascension, then, is not an exaltation to a place he never was before, as if it were some kind of promotion or a reward, his ascension is a return to his former place and a restoration of his original status. Finally, after he was willing to submit to the Father's will, now humanity will submit to him, bowing down in worship and confessing that he is divine. The submission and service that constitutes worship of God is now extended to include Jesus. Therefore, the exaltation of Christ is not simply an ascent granted to Jesus as a reward for his virtue, but the restoration of his original place following a voluntary descent and humiliation. Jesus is not worshiped because he became divine but because he was always divine.

The "name above every name" is the divine name. While the following line ("at the name of Jesus") might lead us to assume that the "name above every name" is simply the name of "Jesus," there is more to it than that. The "name above every name" is meant to evoke the idea of the divine name of God which could not be spoken. When the Scriptures were read in the synagogue, if one came across the divine name in the text, one was expected to substitute the word *Adonai*, which means "Lord" (this is the case in some of our Old Testament passages which mention the Holy Spirit, such as Isaiah 40:13). The designation, "Lord," then took on the meaning of a divine title. But as we have seen in our examination of 1 Corinthians 8:6, in the early Church the title "Lord" came to be used of Christ (Matthew 12:8), which served both to indicate his divinity on one hand and distinguish him from the Father on the other. In fact this would become Paul's favorite term for Christ. Therefore, the "name above every name" is the name "Lord" as it was applied to Jesus. As we have seen, Jesus himself gave us the new substitution for the divine name as it refers to the first person of the Trinity, which is *Abba*, or Father (Matthew 6:9, Romans 8:15, Galatians 4:6). So in the apostolic Church, the God revealed in the Old Testament came to be called the Father, and Jesus came to be called the Lord, just as we see in 1 Corinthians 8:6.

There are other quotations of hymns in the Pauline letters, including Ephesians 5:14 (another stanza of this hymn is preserved in Clement of Alexandria's *Exhortation to the Greeks*, chapter 9), as well as 1 Timothy 3:1 and 2 Timothy 2:11–13. There are also hymn fragments in other New Testament documents, possibly including Hebrews 1:2–4, 12:1–2, 1 Peter 1:20, 2:22–24, 3:18, 22 and John 1:1–5, 9–11, 14. Finally, there seems to be an early hymn quotation in Ignatius of Antioch's *Letter to the Ephesians* 19:2–3, written in the early second century. These repeat the themes we have explored in our two examples, with the addition of specific references to the resurrection and the atonement. We will look at the prologue to John's Gospel when we examine what the Apostle John said about the Trinity, below. For now it is enough to summarize the Trinitarian theology in the early hymns as reflecting the life of Christ in terms of the three phases of his life: preexistence, Incarnation, and exaltation. In his preexistence, Christ was the divine agent of creation, the one through whom all things were created. He is, always and from eternity past, equal to the Father in divinity. However, in his Incarnation, he voluntarily humbled himself and accepted a human nature. As a representative of humanity, he suffered humiliation and death as an atonement for the sins of humanity. In his exaltation, he was raised from death, ascended and restored to his rightful place, vindicated as the one who deserves to be called "Lord." In this way, he claims victory over all other (supposed) powers and even over death itself. This confirms that it is appropriate to worship Jesus Christ.

At the end of his quotation of the hymn in Philippians 2, the Apostle Paul added the words, "to the glory of God the Father," to clarify that there is no competition between the Father and Son; and in fact that it is the Father's will that we worship the Son. However, this serves to highlight once again the paradoxical nature of the relationship of the Father and the Son. The fact that worshiping the Son is acceptable because it is another way of worshiping the Father demonstrates the unity and equality of Father and Son. Yet the fact that the Son was incarnate and the Father was not, that the Son was humbled and subsequently exalted when the Father was not, demonstrates the distinction between Father and Son.

It is interesting to realize that in the earliest decades of the Church, before any of the Christian Scriptures had been written, these hymns, along with any of the prayers or statements of faith that also may have been written down, had already begun the process of explaining the Church's beliefs about Christ and the Trinity. As certain hymns were affirmed by the Church and its leaders, they would no doubt be passed around and shared from city to city, much like the popular worship music of today is heard in one place and brought to another. In this way, the hymns that stood the test of time came to be memorized, thus teaching theology to a Church that didn't yet have a New Testament (Colossians 3:16, Ephesians 5:19). As time went on the hymns probably gained a certain authority as they were more or less universally accepted. This would have allowed Paul to quote them and assume that his audience would not only be familiar with them, but also accept their content as representing the theology of the apostolic Church. Finally, simply being quoted by Paul would give the hymns an even greater credibility and authority, as they became part of sacred Scripture.

Jesus as Lord. As we have seen, the title "Lord" was a substitution for the divine name in Hebrew worship, and as such, it implied divine status. When applied to Jesus, it was an affirmation of his divine nature and his unity with the Father. But the title "Lord" also served to distinguish the Son from the Father, so that there would be no confusion. The title does not imply that the Son is the Father, nor does it imply that the Son is a second God or a competitor for the worship of the one God (*CCC* 202).

John the Baptist had come to "prepare the way of the Lord," (Matthew 3:3, Mark 1:3, Luke 3:4, quoting Isaiah 40:3 and Malachi 3:1), except that now "the Lord" is Jesus. To "call on the name of the Lord" (Joel 3:5/2:32, Psalm 116) came to mean calling on the name of Jesus (Acts 2:17–21, Romans 10:13). By the time of the letters of Paul, this title has become arguably the most important title for Jesus Christ.

By calling Christ "Lord," certain assumptions which were previously associated with God the Father, now become transferred to Christ. These include the ability to heal, cast out demons, to forgive sins, and offer eternal life (John 1:4, Acts 2:38, 10:43, 13:38–39, see Romans 10:9–13). What is more, the concept of the "Day of the Lord" is now understood as the "Day of Christ," or the return (Second Coming) of Jesus (1 Corinthians 5:5, 1 Thessalonians 5:2, 2 Peter 3:10). In the Old Testament, the "Day of the Lord," was the expected time when God would intervene in human history and all wrongs would be righted. The oppressed would be liberated and the oppressors would be punished. For the righteous, the Day of the Lord meant vindication, but for the unrighteous, it meant judgment (see for example Isaiah 13:6–9, Ezekiel 30:3, Amos 5:18–20, Obadiah 1:15, see also 1 Enoch 1:9). The expectation of the Day of the Lord was that God was going to come to the aid of his people. In Christ, God did come to his people, however Jesus did not bring judgment at his first advent. While the Church always believed that the arrival of Christ was the fulfillment of Old Testament promises, he did not in fact fulfill all the promises, so the Church accepted what Jesus himself said—that the remaining promises would be fulfilled at his return. The fact that it is Jesus Christ who will bring judgment highlights his unity with the Father and his divine nature.

The Two Natures of Christ. In some of his letters, Paul was writing to correct what he believed to be mistaken perceptions of Christ. As we can see from the controversies apparent in the letters, it is clear that there were those who taught alternative interpretations of the person of Christ, which were seen by Paul as deviations from the received tradition and apostolic consensus, as well as from his own inspired understanding. Specifically, we can see evidence of the so-called Judaizers, especially in the Letter to the Galatians. From what we can tell, these Judaizers probably denied the divinity of Christ and treated him as though he were a mere human, though perhaps a prophet. We can also see evidence of a group called docetics, especially in 1 Corinthians and Colossians. Docetism was a philosophy based on a strict dualism which said that the spiritual realm (which is good) could not come into contact with the material world (which is evil). When applied to christology, this led to the assumption that Jesus Christ could not have been human, but only appeared to be. The word *docetism* comes from a Greek verb meaning, "to seem," or "to appear." Therefore, the docetics denied the real humanity of Christ, saying that he was only a phantom, or perhaps an angel. They may have considered him divine, but they may also have considered all angels divine and worshiped them as well (Colossians 2:8, 18).

Against the Judaizers, Paul emphasized the spirit over the flesh (the law), and implied that it was the divinity of Christ that allowed him to go beyond the law, to an atonement that would lead to reconciliation with God through the death of the sinless one on the cross. In other words, how could the One who works miracles and reconciles humanity to God be thought to be a mere human? (Galatians 3:1–5). Against the docetics, Paul emphasized the real humanity of Christ, and the fact that it was his humanity that allowed him to give his life for our sins (Colossians 2:12–14). In both cases, Paul draws his readers' attention to the cross and shows how our salvation would not be possible without both the divinity and humanity of Jesus. The one in whom all the fullness of deity dwelt in a human body (Colossians 2:9) is also the one who was able to give his life and die for sinners (Galatians 2:21). Thus the affirmation of the two natures of Christ, divine and human, is articulated against groups who wanted to deny or diminish one nature or the other.

Paul on the Holy Spirit. Just as Jesus had taught, Paul wrote that the Holy Spirit was a gift given by Christ to his followers. According to Paul, the Holy Spirit is both the Spirit of the Father and the Spirit of the Son (Romans 8:9). If the person of Christ is the presence of God dwelling in the world (John 1:14), the Holy Spirit is the presence of God dwelling in believers (1 Corinthians 3:16, 6:19, 2 Timothy 1:14, see 1 Samuel 16:13, Isaiah 44:3, Ezekiel 36:26–28, 37:14, Micah 3:8). In the Church and in the sacraments, it is the indwelling of the Holy Spirit which seals us as God's own people, thus connecting us to the Father and the Son (Ephesians 1:13–14, 4:30). Just as Jesus is called *Christ*, which means The Anointed One, we are *Christ*ians because we are indwelt with same Holy Spirit with whom he was anointed. We are identified with Christ through his Spirit, which leads to our regeneration and salvation (Romans 8:9–17, 1 Corinthians 6:11, Titus 3:5).

In the Christian life, the Holy Spirit within us creates a connection with the Trinity that becomes a channel for receiving peace and joy (Romans 14:17, 1 Thessalonians 1:6), as well as hope (Romans 15:13). It is through the Holy Spirit that the love of God is "poured out into our hearts" (Romans 5:5, see also Galatians 4:6). As Christians, the Holy Spirit informs our conscience (Romans 9:1, see 1 John 4:2) and enables us to grow in holiness (Romans 15:16). The Holy Spirit empowers us to be witnesses to the gospel (1 Thessalonians 1:5, 4:8, 1 Corinthians 12:3, see 2 Corinthians 3:3), and the Holy Spirit empowers us to minister to others through the granting of spiritual gifts (1 Corinthians 12:12–20, see Isaiah 11:2–3).

Finally, the close connection of our own spirit with the Holy Spirit within us means that God knows us and our needs, to the point where prayer does not necessarily require the right words, since the Holy Spirit (as our Advocate) will intercede with the Father on our behalf (Romans 8:26–27). All of this points to the reality that the Holy Spirit is not simply an attribute of God, or a metaphor for the activity of God. The Holy Spirit is *active* in the world and in our lives. In other words, the Holy Spirit is a distinct personal manifestation of divine intervention (Philippians 1:19). Thus the teaching of Paul set the stage for the later clarification of the full divine personhood of the Spirit.

Summary of What Paul Said About the Trinity. In the time before Paul's letters were written, the Church's conviction that it was appropriate, in fact imperative, for Christians to worship Christ led to the beginnings of the explanation of the Trinity, in the form of statements of faith and hymns. By the time Paul was writing his letters, though the Church was only a few decades old, there was already a sense that there was an established tradition (1 Corinthians 15:3, see 1 Corinthians 11:23). Even though Paul would claim that his gospel comes directly from Christ, he certainly would not want to teach anything contrary to what the other apostles were teaching. Therefore, Pauline theology accepts the conclusions of the pre-Pauline period but explains and expands upon them.

As Paul responded to various alternative views about the person and mission of Christ, he was actually helping the Church to define, not only its theology, but its very identity. What Paul saw as incorrect beliefs about Christ and his relationship to the Father prompted him to explain his own understanding of the Trinity, theology that he would argue was more consistent with the convictions of the other apostles and with the teaching and worship of the Church in the previous decades.

Therefore the Apostle Paul represents the beginning of the process of interpreting the person and teachings of Jesus, in an attempt to understand him and explain his relationship to the

Father. That relationship is articulated in terms of both unity and distinction. The unity of Father and Son was described as an equality of divine nature and unified activity. The use of the title "Lord" for Jesus implies his divine status, as well as his mission of doing the work of the Father. To make the distinction between the Father and the Son, the term "God" was normally reserved for the Father. The distinction between Father and Son was further described using the concepts of Source versus agent, sender versus messenger, and by the fact that only the Son was incarnate.

The Son is mediator of both creation and redemption. His two natures are evidenced in his preexistence (divinity) and suffering (humanity). His voluntary death and resurrection make our salvation possible, and his passion is continually re-enacted in the sacraments of baptism and the Eucharist (1 Corinthians 11:26). Finally, the Holy Spirit is the gift and presence of the Father and Son indwelling believers.

What John Said About the Trinity

The Gospel of John has often been described as an example of so-called "high" christology. However, as I have already indicated, such labels are at best unhelpful and at worst misleading. The label implies that the christology of the Gospel of John emphasizes the divinity of Christ more than the humanity (or at least emphasizes Christ's divinity more than perhaps some other New Testament documents). However, if that were true, it would imply that the Johannine community leaned toward the heresy of docetism, which denied or diminished Christ's true humanity. In fact, there is actually an emphasis in the Johannine literature to combat docetism and argue for the full humanity of Christ. Apparently there had been some docetics in the Johannine community, but by the time the First Letter of John was written, they had left the community because they did not believe in the true humanity of Christ (1 John 2:18-19, 4:1-6). The Johannine literature, like the Pauline, is neither "high" nor "low" in its christology but emphasizes the Incarnation in such a way that it maintains both Christ's full divinity and his true humanity.

Jesus as the Word of God. In the prologue to the Gospel of John (John 1:1-18), Jesus is called the Word, or the *Logos*, in Greek. This term did not originate with John, in fact there are some who believe that the prologue itself is a quotation of a hymn, like the hymns quoted in Paul's letters. The concept of the *Logos*, as it is applied to Christ by John, is actually the combination of two streams of thought—one Jewish and one Greek.

In Jewish thought, sometimes God's wisdom was personified, as it is in Proverbs 8:22-31. Note how in this passage, wisdom is speaking in the first person and is presented as an eternal (preexistent) expression of God. Wisdom even claims to participate in the creation of the world (see Psalm 33:6). In later Jewish literature, wisdom is described in stronger terms as the agent of creation and is even called the image of God (for example, see Wisdom 7:22-26, 9:1-2, Sirach 24:1-9). Also, in the apocryphal book of 1 Enoch, the wisdom of God is described as being rejected in ways that parallel John 1:12: "Wisdom came to make its dwelling place among the children of men, but found no dwelling place" (1 Enoch 42:2). Of course personified wisdom was not thought to become incarnate, it was in reality only an attribute of God, not really distinct from God. However, when these various concepts of personified wisdom are taken together, we can see that in Hebrew wisdom literature there were at least some precedents for a divine agent of creation that is described as distinct from God the Father.

At the same time, Greek philosophy had come to believe in a rational "matrix" underlying creation that came to be thought of as the soul of the world. Plato related this world "soul" to the philosophical concept of *logos*, which is a Greek term with a range of meaning, including "word," "saying," "reason," or "rationality," but can also have the connotation of, "order," "harmony," and "proportion." It is where we get our English word, "logic," and the suffix, "-ology." The philosophical concept of the *logos* was thought to be spiritual, but created. It was divinely ordered but not actually divine. It was understood to be the structure that sustains creation, rather like the frame of a building. It holds the building together, but it is still part of the building.

Philo of Alexandria, a Jewish philosopher, combined aspects of personified wisdom with the philosophical *logos*. For him, the *logos* is divine, but it is not God. Although it is described as quasi-divine, it is still created and impersonal. It seems Philo had accepted what most Christian philosophers would not—the possibility of degrees of divinity. If Plato's *logos* was like the frame of a building (the structure of creation but still part of creation), we might think of Philo's *logos* as not only the frame of the building but also the blueprint of the building (having as much to do with the design of creation that exists in the mind of God). It is interesting to note that Jewish and Greek thinkers alike were looking for a way to talk about a connection between humanity (creation) and the Divine (the Creator). In both cases, this led to speculation about a mediator of some kind. However, while the philosophers wrote about a mediator who was somewhere *between* the Creator and creation, the Church affirmed that its mediator, Jesus Christ, is *both* fully divine and fully human.

In the prologue to the fourth gospel, the concepts of personified wisdom and the philosophical *logos* are appropriated as a way to describe Christ. It is as if using this term for Christ was meant to be acceptable to both Jews and gentiles. To the Jews, Christ as *Logos* is like God's wisdom, the preexistent agent of creation, but who then becomes the human embodiment of God's word. To the Greeks, Christ as *Logos* is like Plato's world soul and Philo's *logos*, the rational "matrix" of creation, but who is also a person, a divine mediator reconciling Creator and creation. Using the analogy of the building, if Plato's *logos* was the frame of the building, and Philo's *logos* was the blueprint of the building, John's *Logos* is the architect of the building (and thus not part of creation).

What was new in the Christian concept of *Logos* was the fact that Jesus Christ is not simply an impersonal manifestation of God's attribute of wisdom, he is a fully divine person, yet distinct from God the Father, the evidence of which is the Incarnation. On the other hand, he is not so distinct from God as to be a part of creation. The Word of God is Divine ("the Word *was* God") and yet the Word of God is not the Father ("the Word was *with* God").

The Gospel of John begins the way Genesis begins, and this is intentional. "In the beginning" means, "at the time of creation" and so Christ is presented as preexistent, or existing before creation (see John 1:15). Just as God created by his word when he said, "Let there be light…" (Genesis 1:3), so the Word of God is the divine agent through whom all things were created (John 1:3, 10). Then, when the *Logos* became flesh (that is, human), the agent of creation is shown to be also the agent of redemption, as the Word of God came into the world to be its Savior (John 1:9, 12–13). The Word became human to reveal the Father to humanity (John 1:14, 18) and to invite humans into the divine light (John 1:9). The themes of light and life in both Genesis and John connect the Word to the Father in a unique and unprecedented way. The Word is the one who brings the light and life of God, which is possible because he has light and life within himself (John 1:4). He can grant these because they are his to give—he is the Source of light and life no less than the Father, because he is divine. The implication here is that it would not be enough for Christ as mediator to stand between God and humanity, or even be half divine and half human; he is both fully divine and fully human, which allows him to give the blessings of his divinity to humanity, in solidarity with humanity.

For John, the preexistent *Logos* "was God" (John 1:1) and is the "only-begotten God" (John 1:18, see also John 3:13; 6:38, 62; 8:23, 42, 58; 17:5). By calling Christ "God," John has gone further than any other New Testament writer in associating Jesus with the divinity of the Father.

Jesus as the Lamb of God. In the Gospel of John, Jesus' ministry begins with the announcement of John the Baptist: "Behold! The Lamb of God, who takes away the sin of the world" (John 1:29, 36). But "Lamb of God" is more than just another name for Jesus, it is a prophetic proclamation that comes true when Jesus is crucified on the same day on which the Passover lambs were slaughtered (John 19:14). Here the death of Christ as atonement combines the two Old Testament concepts of the Passover lamb (Exodus 12, see Genesis 22:8) and the Day of Atonement scapegoat (Leviticus 16:9–10). So the concept of Jesus as Lamb of God is more than just a reminder of the lamb of the exodus, it combines the Passover and the Day of Atonement into one "package," which means that Jesus' death is the atoning sacrifice "for our sins" (1 John 2:2, 4:10, see Leviticus 16:21–22, Isaiah 53:4–5). He "takes away the sin of the world" just as the animal sacrifices of the Old Testament were believed to erase the sins of the people and give them a clean slate. He is the agent of the Father's salvation precisely because he is the sacrifice that makes forgiveness possible. In other words, "Lamb of God" means "Lamb of the Father."

It is important to note, however, that Jesus is not a helpless victim. His divine nature makes it impossible that he could die against his will, therefore his death is voluntary. This is connected to the idea of the lamb led to the slaughter without complaining (Isaiah 53:7) and is expressed in the fourth gospel by Jesus' statement that he will lay down his life, no one will take it from him (John 10:17–18). Note that in the pre-Pauline hymn quoted in Philippians 2, Jesus' death is described as humbling himself (Philippians 2:8). Therefore, the atoning death of Christ has one very important difference from the lamb of the Passover and the scapegoat. Jesus has chosen to die for us, and while death has come at the hands of his enemies, it has not been forced on him. The voluntary nature of the passion of Christ is important as a response to contemporary critiques of atonement theology, critiques which attempt to describe the traditional theories of atonement as a form of injustice on the part of the Father. Though we may say that the Father gave his only Son to die for us (John 3:16), it is equally true that the Son gave his own life, of his own free will, and that his sacrifice for us is actually an act of love (John 15:13). Although it is not included in the Johannine account, we can see the conformity of Jesus' human will to the divine will in his prayer in the Garden of Gethsemane, "not my will, but yours be done..." (Luke 22:42, see Matthew 26:42, Mark 14:36, John 6:38).

Even the resurrection is presented in John as an "auto-resurrection." While the other gospels speak of the Son being raised by the Father (Matthew 17:22–23, 20:18–20), in the fourth gospel Jesus says he will raise himself (John 10:17–18). No doubt both ways of understanding the resurrection are true (based on the unity of Father and Son), but in John, the ability to raise himself from death is evidence of Jesus' divine nature, as demonstrated in his power over death itself.

As the Father's revelation, the Son brings God (divinity) to humanity, and those who have seen him have (in a way) seen the Father (John 14:9, see John 1:14–18). In Thomas' confession, "my

Lord and my God" (John 20:28), we hear an echo of the divine titles demanded by the emperor, and the reader is reminded that it is Christ, not the emperor, who is worthy of worship.

The Johannine Trinity. By the time the Book of Revelation was written, the Church had a longstanding tradition of the worship of Christ, yet it is clear that worship was still something guarded and reserved for God alone. Note that Jesus is worshiped (Revelation 5:8–9), but angels are not (Revelation 19:10, 22:8–9). This assumes the divinity of Christ, however it still begs the larger question of the relationship of Christ to the (monotheistic) God of the Old Testament.

As the Son of the Father, Christ is both equal to the Father and not equal to the Father. He is equal to the Father in terms of his divinity, especially as it is revealed in his role as Creator and Source of life. As agent of creation, the Son is no less Creator than the Father. In this sense, the Word of God *is* God (John 1:1). Christ's relationship to the Holy Spirit is also evidence of his divinity and his equality with the Father. In the fourth gospel, the Father gives the Spirit (John 14:16, 26), but it can also be said that the Son gives the Spirit (John 15:26, 16:7). Therefore as the co-sender of the Holy Spirit, the Son is equal to the Father. Note that in Revelation 14:1, the mark of God on the foreheads of the faithful is the name of both the Father and the Son.

The equality of the Father and the Son is also seen in the concept of divine sonship. While we have already examined the implications of the titles "Son of God" and "Son of Man," there remains the question of how we as humans might be sons and daughters of God, as well as how this is the same as or different from the sonship of Jesus. John explains this using the concept of adoption. As the divine Word, Jesus is the "natural" Son of God, that is, he is the Son of God by nature, therefore he is unique among humanity in his relationship to God. This is what it means that Jesus is the "only begotten" Son of God (John 1:14, 18; 3:16–18; 1 John 4:9). We can become sons and daughters of God by adoption, by accepting the natural Son of God as our brother (John 1:12–13, see Romans 8:14–25). In this way, we can become co-heirs of God with Christ and share in his inheritance of eternal life. In fact, the indwelling of the Holy Spirit is the down payment on that inheritance (1 John 3:24, 4:13, see Romans 8:11, 1 Corinthians 6:19). So while we can be adopted sons and daughters of God, only Christ is the Son of God by nature.

At the same time, there are ways in which the Son is not equal to the Father. There is a hierarchy within the Trinity, and while we must maintain that all three persons of the Trinity are equal in divinity, each divine person has a position relative to the others that is based on the concept of sending. The Father sent the Son, which makes the Son the Father's messenger (John 1:18, 8:26, 15:15). As the early theologians pointed out, the Sender has a priority of authority over the Messenger. This is based on the fact that the Father alone is the First Cause. It is the Sender's message that the Messenger brings. To put it another way, it is the Sender's authority which the Messenger enforces. In the same way, the Holy Spirit is sent by both the Father and the Son (John 14:16, 26; 15:26; 16:7), which places the Son between the Father and the Spirit in the hierarchy. Therefore, the Son is equal to the Father and the Spirit in terms of divinity, and yet on the other hand, both the Son and the Spirit are not equal to the Father in terms of their relationship to each other.

This is not to imply that the three persons of the Trinity can be described by function or "job description." Terms such as "sender" and "messenger" are primarily relational and are only meant to describe our perception of the relationship between the persons of the Trinity, not the persons themselves and not the relationship of divine persons to humanity (*CCC* 252, 255). The point is that there is a hierarchy assumed between the persons of the Trinity so that while the persons are equal according to their divinity and their very being ("the Father and I are one," John 10:30), there is still a distinction of authority between the persons ("the Father is greater than I," John 14:28). Another way to say this is that the Father and Son are unified in divinity ("the Word *was* God"), but they are not identical ("the Word was *with* God"). They are unified in activity (inseparable operation), but not identical in authority (the Father alone is First Cause, the ultimate Source, and Sender of the Son and Spirit). Thus we can see in the Johannine literature the development of an understanding of the balance of unity and distinction within the Trinity. The persons of the Trinity are not separate, but they are distinct.

Therefore the Johannine Trinity goes beyond simply naming the three persons in a blessing or liturgical formula, such as we saw in the Great Commission passage (Matthew 28:19) or in the benedictions of the Pauline letters. The Johannine Trinity exhibits a more advanced understanding of the three persons and the relationships between them. In the Johannine literature, especially as it finds its culmination in the book of Revelation, the Trinity is described in this way: The Father is the *One Who Sits on the Throne* (Revelation 5:13, 6:16, 7:10) and the one who sends the Son and the Spirit into the world. The Son is the *Word of God* who became human, but also the *Lamb Who Was Slain*— slain and yet now stands raised (Revelation 5:6–12, 13:8). This Lamb is worshiped with the singing of a new song, the song of the new covenant (Revelation 5:12, 14:3). The Son is worshiped along with the Father and with the Father sends the Spirit to the Church. The Holy Spirit is described as the "sevenfold" (that is, omnipresent and omniscient) Spirit of God (Revelation 1:4, 3:1, 4:5, 5:6). The Spirit is the gift of the Father and the Son and is the down payment on our inheritance as adopted sons and daughters of God. From this is it clear that the three persons of the Trinity (though they are not yet called "persons" and God is not yet called a "Trinity") are understood as distinct divine entities. The Father, Son, and Spirit are "God," and yet they are not simply three names for the one God, nor are they three Gods. They are in fact three manifestations of God that nevertheless do not compromise the oneness of God. Put another way, monotheism is being redefined (or reinterpreted) to include distinction within the unity.

Summary of What John Said About the Trinity. In the Johannine literature, Christ is both *Logos* and Lamb. As *Logos*, or Word of God, he is the preexistent agent of creation, which means that he is Creator. He is also described as the Source of life (John 1:4). On one level, this means life in general, so that to say he is the Source of life is the same as saying he is Creator. On another level, it also means that he is the Source of eternal life. As Lamb, his death is a voluntary sacrifice of atonement for the reconciliation of humanity with the Father.

The Son is one with the Father (John 10:30), yet is not the Father (John 14:28). He is divine, yet distinct from the Father (but not so distinct as to be separate from the Divine and part of creation). He is eternal, yet incarnate. He is not between divinity and humanity, nor is he half divine and half human, he is both fully divine and truly human. The Son is equal in divinity with the Father and the Spirit and unified in activity, and yet there is a hierarchy of authority within the Trinity. The Son is the messenger of the Father, and co-sender of the Holy Spirit with the Father.

Summary

At this stage, the Church's understanding of the Trinity is only developed insofar as it relates to what can be gleaned from the teachings of Jesus and the writings of the apostles. In some cases I have looked ahead to the ways in which these biblical texts would be interpreted by the Church. At the end of the day, we have to admit that while we may be able to see the Trinity in the text of Scripture, the *doctrine* of the Trinity is not in Scripture, *per se*, but is the result of the Church's interpretation of Scripture.

According to Jesus' own teaching as recorded in the gospels, the God of the Old Testament is to be called "Father," which carries the meaning of Creator, Provider, Protector and Redeemer. Jesus referred to himself as the Son, usually Son of Man, which was a deliberate reference to the vision of Daniel 7. This connection was interpreted as early evidence of Christ's divinity and preexistence. In his teaching and in his life, death and resurrection, Jesus redefined the concept of Messiah to include vicarious suffering (Isaiah 53), and the Church would take his comments about the Temple to mean that he was replacing the Temple as the focal point of God's presence on earth. He claimed to have authority to forgive sins, something only God can do, and by his teaching and example he implied that he came with the Father's authority.

In the Pauline literature, the two natures of Christ's divinity and humanity are affirmed against alternative teachings that would deny one or the other. In his divine nature, Christ is preexistent and equal to the Father. In his human nature, he was incarnate, suffered, and died for our sins. His Incarnation is a descent to the human realm, and his ascension is a restoration to his prior state of exaltation. The Holy Spirit indwells believers and so is a manifestation of the presence of God yet is also distinct from the Father and the Son.

In the Johannine witness, we read that the Son is Creator. He is the agent, heir, and messenger of the Father. Jesus' pre-existence is evidence of his divinity, and his Incarnation demonstrates his humanity. The fact that he was incarnate and the Father was not is further evidence of a distinction between persons that was understood to have existed even before the Incarnation (based on the "Angel of the Lord" appearances). The Son is one with the Father, but not the same as the Father. The Son is our Advocate with the Father, and the Holy Spirit is another Advocate, whom the Father and Son send to the Church.

As the theologians of the first and second centuries examined and interpreted the Scriptures, they came to the conclusion that there was both unity and distinction in the Trinity. The unity is in the equal (that is, singular) divinity and inseparable operation (that all three persons of the Trinity are at work in all divine activity). The practical application of belief in this unity was the conviction that it is appropriate to worship Jesus Christ.

The distinction is in the hierarchy of authority, that is, the relationships of Sender and Messenger among the persons of the Trinity. Since the Father cannot be circumscribed (localized/visible/tangible), the Son must be the Father's messenger on earth. The Son comes with the Father's authority, but defers to it. Just as the Father sends the Son, the Father and Son send the Holy Spirit. However, to keep this in perspective, we must remember that from the human point of view all three persons of the Trinity together constitute one divine authority.

To summarize, the early Christians put together all of the above-mentioned Scripture passages and determined that God was being described in the Scriptures as three distinct manifestations who nevertheless are together the one God. Though the doctrine of the Trinity was far from formalized or universally understood, the early Christians could say that Scripture pointed to the threefold revelation of God:

God the Father (equivalent to Yahweh, the God of the Old Testament)

God as Father means Creator-Parent (Isaiah 64:8)

God as Father means Savior-Protector (Exodus 15:1–18, Isaiah 63:16)

The Son of God (Jesus Christ, the promised Messiah, the Word/*Logos* of God)

The Concept of Messiah was reinterpreted to include suffering (Isaiah 53)

Christians interpreted Jesus' life, ministry and death in light of Isaiah:

The Son is one with the Father (Isaiah 7:14, 9:6, John 10:30)

The Son comes with the Father's authority (Isaiah 9:6–7, Matthew 21:37)

The Son is divine presence (Isaiah 7:14, Matthew 18:20, John 1:14)

Jesus associated himself with Yahweh/Abba in a unique relationship:

Matthew 16:13–20 (connecting himself also with Daniel 7:13–14)

Matthew 28:16–20

Luke 10:16, 12:8–9

John 14:6–29, 15:6 (see also Acts 4:12)

The Holy Spirit (the "Spirit of the Lord")

The Spirit is the inspiration of the prophets and the apostles

The Spirit is the presence of God within believers

The Holy Spirit is the Spirit of the Father

The Holy Spirit is the Spirit of Christ (John 16:7–15, Romans 8:9)

DISCUSSION QUESTIONS

1. What are the three ways that people use the word God, and how is it properly used of Jesus Christ?

2. Why is it appropriate to call all three persons of the Trinity "Creator"? What is the doctrine of "inseparable operation"?

3. What are the three phases of the life of Christ? What does it mean that Jesus Christ is preexistent?

4. What do Jesus' own baptism and his words on baptism at the end of the Gospel of Matthew teach us about the Trinity?

5. What do the titles "Son of God" and "Son of Man" imply about Jesus Christ?

6. Why was it considered appropriate by early Christians to worship Jesus Christ?

7. What does it mean that Jesus Christ is the "agent" of creation, and the "agent" of redemption?

8. What does it mean that Christ "emptied himself" to become incarnate and human? What does it not mean?

9. In what ways are the Father and the Son one? In what ways are the Father and the Son distinct?

10. What are some of the biblical concepts that point to the divinity of Christ?

CHAPTER 2

The Doctrine of the Trinity

The Problem Faced by the First Christians

Imagine yourself a member of a Jewish family in the first century. You have come to be convinced that Jesus of Nazareth is the Messiah your people have hoped for and you've been baptized into the community of his followers. Now imagine that you're at a family gathering and one of your relatives asks you, "What do you and those others do when you gather at dawn on Sunday mornings?" And you respond sheepishly, "We...uh...we worship Jesus...."

"You what?" would no doubt be the reply. And at that point the whole family gathered around the table would descend on you with exclamations like, "You're a child of Abraham! You can't do that!" "Don't you know the law? Worship only God!" "How can you turn your back on your faith?" And so on. To be fair, they would have a point. The one most important hallmark of Judaism (if I may venture to say, speaking as a gentile) is that there is only one God and only the one God should be worshiped (Deuteronomy 6:4). The one God is all-sufficient and does not need any other gods to be the Creator and Sustainer of the universe. And yet the experience of the risen Christ led the early Christian believers to the conviction that they should worship Jesus—they must worship Jesus—and in fact, worshiping Jesus somehow was worshiping God. The problem was not a lack of conviction that they were doing the right thing in worshiping Jesus. The problem was that they didn't quite know how to explain it within the context of a monotheistic religion. In other words, how do you justify the worship of Jesus and still claim to believe in only one God? This is the problem of Christian monotheism. In fact, one could argue that "Christian monotheism" seems like a contradiction in terms, a bit like saying, "kosher bacon." So how do you reconcile the apparent contradiction? The solution to this problem is what we call the doctrine of the Trinity.

The first task of Christian theology, then, was to redefine monotheism to include Jesus. In other words, to give an account of the doctrine of God that maintains conformity with monotheism, yet in light of the experience of the death and resurrection of Jesus. But there was a major stumbling block in the way, something that was a deal-breaker for most Jewish believers. Jesus was executed. The Old Testament has a saying, "God's curse rests on him who hangs on a tree." Since only criminals were executed, it was assumed that anyone executed must be a criminal. It was thought, therefore, that such a person was rejected by God. For the average observer of the events of Jesus' life, it would mean that he could not be the Messiah, since a crucified messiah would have been considered an insurmountable contradiction (see Paul's answer to the problem in Galatians 3:13). While there was a diversity of opinion on the nature of the Messiah in first-century Judaism, most people who were expecting a Messiah did not expect one who would suffer, let alone die. For any who might have expected the Messiah to be divine in any sense, this was even more problematic.

To both the Hebrew and the Greek mind, God cannot suffer, because suffering is a form of change, and God cannot change. Put another way, for Jews and for Greek philosophers alike, the very definition of divinity includes divine impassibility and divine immutability: the Divine cannot suffer and the Divine cannot change (Malachi 3:6). This logically follows from the assumption of God's perfection. Any kind of change would negate perfection, because a God who changed either became perfect from a state of less than perfection; or worse, a perfect God who could change might become less than perfect. In other words, divine perfection (holiness) requires divine immutability.

Therefore, the early Christians' belief that Jesus was divine and worthy of worship was offensive to both Jews and gentiles (1 Corinthians 1:23). Jews did not believe that a crucified man could be the Messiah, let alone a divine person. And they certainly would not accept that a human being should be worshiped. Pagans did not believe that a divine being could take on flesh and suffer. So they would assume that any being worthy of worship could not have suffered and died. These assumptions on the part of Jews and pagans would lead to alternative ways of understanding Christ, the seeds of which have already been seen in the New Testament and which would in turn evolve into the major heresies of the early Church. So the Incarnation—the belief that a divine being became flesh and suffered death—was a problem for everyone, including the Christians who had to try to explain it to people.

For the Christians, worshiping Jesus did not amount to a rejection of monotheism. On the contrary, worshiping Jesus was as good as worshiping God the Father. So they continued singing songs to Jesus, praying for his presence and intervention in their lives, and celebrating the Eucharist. In fact, as we have seen, they found examples in the New Testament that supported the worship of Jesus (Matthew 2:2–11, 14:33, 28:17; John 9:35–38; Philippians 2:9–11).

However, non-Christian Jews, and even some within the Church, remained uncomfortable with the worship of Jesus and continued asking the tough questions of Christian monotheism. As we will see, in an attempt to protect monotheism, alternative explanations of the person of Christ emerged that would force the mainstream Church to further define orthodox christology.

PAPANDREA'S THREE LAWS OF EARLY CHRISTIAN DOCTRINE

As I always tell my students, there are three observable laws of the development of doctrine in early Christianity. They are really more like generalizations discerned in retrospect than laws, but they are helpful for studying and understanding the theology of the early Church. My students know them as "Papandrea's Three Laws." The three laws are:

1. Heresy forces orthodoxy to define itself.
2. Orthodoxy is the middle way between the extreme alternatives.
3. Christology informs soteriology.

The first law is that *heresy forces orthodoxy to define itself.* It is an observable phenomenon that the early Christians did not intentionally begin to define the boundaries of correct belief until the mainstream Church was faced with competing interpretations. This process begins in the letters of Paul, as we have already seen. Paul was not trying to write a systematic theology, he was simply responding to challenges, one issue at a time. Thus the early Church's clarification of correct belief (orthodoxy) was defined in opposition to alternative teachings that were determined to be incompatible with the Church's experience, its received tradition, and with the whole witness of Scripture.

This is not to say that heresy precedes orthodoxy, or that orthodoxy was in any way dependent on, or derivative of, heresy. In fact since the orthodox position in every generation was consistent with the conclusions of the previous generation, it would have been argued that heresy was a deviation from those previously accepted conclusions. However, the Church was not forced to *define* orthodoxy in clear terms until multiple (and mutually exclusive) interpretive options presented themselves. At each stage of the development of doctrine, the majority of the bishops of the Church responded to what they saw as deviations from the conclusions of the previous stage and responded by defining the boundaries of correct belief specifically to exclude those deviations.

There is a corollary to the first law, which is that in the earliest decades of the life of the Church it is also the case that liturgy forced orthodoxy to define itself. As we have seen, from the very beginning of the Church, Christians were convinced that worshiping Christ was God's will. Even the Roman persecutors of the Church knew that Christians worshiped Christ "as a god." This worship included the singing of hymns to Christ, praying for Christ's presence and intervention in life, reciting creeds or statements of faith that make Christ the object of faith, and conducting sacraments in the name of Christ. The practice was well-established before it was ever formally justified, but it was the early Christians' need to defend the practice in the face of Jewish objection that forced them to start thinking about how monotheism would require some redefinition in light of Jesus Christ.

The second law of early Christian doctrine is that ***orthodoxy is the middle way between the extreme alternatives***. Another way to say this is that there is a center of gravity where truth resides—a place of balance between the mutually exclusive extremes at the fringes. As we will see, the heresies were interpretations that focused on one aspect of Christ and his relationship to the Father while ignoring another. Often this meant that they each emphasized certain Scripture passages about Christ while discounting others. For the orthodox mainstream, it will not be enough to speak of the humanity of Jesus only, or the divinity only, but both must be affirmed. In effect, the arguments of the various heresies cancel each other out, while the orthodox position presents a middle way, refusing to avoid paradox and refusing to discount any biblical texts.

The third law of early Christian doctrine is that **christology informs soteriology**. Soteriology is the understanding of salvation, and whatever one believes about Jesus Christ will affect what one believes about salvation and the atonement. It also works the other way, so that if one begins with an assumption about salvation and/or atonement, that assumption will push a person in one direction or another with regard to beliefs about Christ and the Trinity. The importance of this law will become clear when we look at the heresy of Arianism and examine its implications for salvation, but for now it is enough to note that this answers the question why some interpretations were considered right and others were considered wrong. The Church could not tolerate a diversity of theologies since it was assumed that souls were at stake. Some interpretations of Christ and the Trinity were considered wrong because they logically led to theories of salvation that are incompatible with the preaching of the gospel. In other words, incorrect christology (believing in the *wrong* christ) would not lead one to salvation, and anyone who taught an incorrect christology was a heretic, not only because he deviated from orthodoxy, but because he was leading people astray and away from God.

Before we go on, we must clarify a couple of definitions. The word "heresy" or "heretic" comes from a Greek word that means to separate, or to go off on one's own. It implies one holds an opinion that diverges from the majority. And, in fact, that is exactly what heresy is. When used in this book, the word "heretic" is not meant to be condescending—in fact, today we assume the sincerity of the heretics, even if their more mainstream Christian contemporaries did not always give them the benefit of the doubt. They were not evil people who wanted to lead innocent Christians astray. They were probably well-meaning believers who passionately held a minority position. I will have more to say about the process by which heresy is discerned, but for now it is enough to say that the recurring pattern is that the majority position won the day and the designation of "heresy" was a label applied by the mainstream majority. Unfortunately, we often don't know very much about the ones who would come to be called heretics. Most of their writings are lost, and what we do know about them comes to us from their opponents so that we have a rough sketch at best, which in the end may not be a fair representation of their teachings. Finally, it must be noted that within the heretical groups there was probably more diversity of thought than agreement, but from what we know we can categorize the heresies into distinct groups, at least for the sake of study.

Just like "heresy," the word "orthodoxy" comes from a Greek word, in this case it is a compound word that literally means "correct praise," but loosely translated it means "correct belief." The orthodox are those who won the debates, in large part because their interpretations were more consistent with the accepted beliefs of previous generations of Church leaders and with the whole witness of Scripture. By defining orthodoxy in opposition to alternatives (heresy), the early writers were defining the boundaries of what would be considered acceptable interpretations of theology. Therefore, it is safe to say that what we call "orthodoxy" represents the mainstream, or the majority, of the Church in any given time period. We will not concern ourselves with making distinctions between "orthodoxy" and "proto-orthodoxy," as if orthodoxy is something that only exists after the Council of Nicaea. There is an orthodoxy at every stage of the Church's life, in which mainstream writers understood their position as correct over against opposing positions which they called heresy. But even more important, the orthodox position is that which is most consistent with previous tradition going back to the apostles, and through them, to Jesus himself.

Therefore, the orthodoxy of any given time period of the early Church was built on the conclusions (the orthodoxy) of the previous generations. In other words, orthodoxy is the "tradition," while heresy is the "innovation." This is partly based on the ancient world's conviction that what is older is always better. Today we live in such a technology-driven age that it's hard for us to imagine such a world view. To us, whatever is newer is always thought to be better. But for the people of the ancient world, whatever had been around longer and had stood the test of time was more trustworthy. Thus the early Christians held the conviction that correct belief in any age was whatever was most consistent with correct belief of previous ages, going back to the apostles, and through them, to Jesus himself. The most reliable teachings come from the Source of truth, Christ. Therefore whatever was perceived as a new idea, or a deviation from the established beliefs, was automatically suspect. This means that for an interpretation to be accepted, it had to be consistent with the interpretations of the past generations of bishops. In fact, the mainstream theologians of the early Church would never have wanted to be perceived as having taught anything that was truly new. They only wanted to clarify the faith of the apostles and correct those whom they believed had gotten it wrong.

The conviction that tradition was more trustworthy than innovation led to the concept of *apostolic succession*. Apostolic succession is based on the assumption that the teachers of any generation were faithfully transmitting what they were taught by the teachers of the previous generation, so that the best way to safeguard the teaching of the Church was to trace the succession of teachers in an unbroken chain going back to Jesus himself. In other words, Jesus' disciples became the apostles, who taught their own disciples, who then became their successors in the leadership of the Church. Those successors, or "elders," as they were called, taught their successors and so on. As the office of bishop evolved, the bishops took on the role of primary teacher (and teaching authority) in each city. This development of a centralized authority in the teaching office of the Church was seen as essential to maintain unity and avoid both heresy and schism. Furthermore, it was of course assumed that the established tradition of the mainstream Church (the *sensus fidelium*) was guided by God. The same Holy Spirit who had inspired the writing of the sacred Scriptures would also inspire the interpretation of those Scriptures and the development of doctrinal tradition.

When it comes to the development of doctrine, the history of the Church is the history of the interpretation of Scripture. When one teacher or group focused on certain Scripture passages to the exclusion of others, or allowed an emphasis on certain philosophical assumptions to influence their reading of Scripture, the result was an interpretation that went to an extreme and ventured outside the boundaries of orthodoxy, boundaries which were set by the conclusions of the previous generation, going back to the apostles. Over time, as the mainstream Church continued to respond to the alternative interpretations of each generation, orthodoxy was defined with increasing clarity.

In the end, orthodoxy would always be defined as a balanced position that refused to reject one part of the truth about Christ in favor of emphasizing another part. It was not a question of either/or, but a balance of both. Christ is not human only, or divine only, but both human and divine. To put it another way, correct belief is expressed in the balance of seemingly paradoxical convictions, thus avoiding the extremes, and holding truths together rather than choosing between them. The mainstream Church was not asking which Scripture passages were true, but how they could all be true together.

ALTERNATIVE ANSWERS TO THE QUESTION

As I noted above, the question that most occupied the minds of the theologians of the first three centuries was the relationship between Jesus Christ (the Son) and the Father. The Church would get around to a more detailed discussion of the Holy Spirit in the fourth century, but for the earliest Church, explaining the problem of Christian monotheism was the most important task. The majority of the bishops implicitly agreed that monotheism itself had to be described in a way that would include the divinity of Christ. This was not a new idea. It goes all the way back to the beginning of the Church, as we see in Paul's quotation of an early Christian affirmation of faith in 1 Corinthians 8:6. However, it was inevitable that some teachers would propose explanations that differed from the majority. These alternative interpretations would come to be labeled heresies.

In the second century, the primary heresies each denied one of the two natures of Christ, his humanity or his divinity. For example, on one extreme there were the christologies that emphasized the humanity of Christ while denying his divinity. This was probably already happening with the Judaizers who opposed Paul, but it was even more clearly exemplified in the second century with a group who called themselves the Ebionites. They believed and taught that Jesus was a prophet who was inspired by the Holy Spirit, but like the prophets of the Old Testament, he was a mere man. As one might expect, the Ebionites accepted Scripture texts that affirmed Jesus' humanity but rejected or allegorized those texts which pointed to his divinity. As an example of what is sometimes called "Jewish Christianity," the Ebionites would have rejected the worship of Christ, since they believed that no human being could be worthy of worship.

On the other extreme, there were the christologies that emphasized the divinity of Christ while denying his true humanity. Those who taught this kind of christology were the docetics, and by the second century, the gnostics. Since they did not believe that a divine being could become human, they diminished the humanity of Christ. The gnostics added to the docetic christology by teaching that the God of the Old Testament was an evil demi-god who was out to get humanity (evidenced by the Flood). For the gnostics, Christ came as a divine spirit to bring secret knowledge that would allow some humans to escape from the material world and be saved from the Old Testament God. The word "gnosticism" comes from the Greek word for knowledge, *gnosis*. This secret knowledge would enlighten the truly spiritual people, making them aware of their own divinity and their relationship to a higher God, the one whom Jesus called his Father. For them the resurrection was only a mystical vision in which Christ was revealed in his true, non-human, form. Thus, salvation was not by atonement but by enlightenment, and those who did not have the secret knowledge could not hope to be saved. The docetics and gnostics, therefore, accepted the Scriptures that spoke of Christ's divinity but rejected those passages that demonstrated his humanity. The gnostics eventually even wrote their own gospels to distinguish themselves from the Church and promote their own theology.

It is interesting to note that among both the Ebionites and gnostics there were those who speculated about a distinction between the man Jesus and the "Christ-spirit." In opposition to this, orthodox bishops such as Irenaeus of Lyons affirmed that we cannot separate the "concepts" of *Jesus* and *Christ*, not even to distinguish his human nature from his divine nature. It is never appropriate to separate Jesus and Christ into two separate entities. Both terms must refer to the one person of Jesus Christ, who is both the Word of God and the man Jesus of Nazareth.

The primary alternative christologies of the third century were forms of *monarchianism*, from the word *monarch*, meaning "one ruler." In other words, both extremes began with the premise that they were protecting monotheism, because they believed that the mainstream Church was teaching a form of polytheism, with the Father and Son (and the Holy Spirit) being worshiped as multiple Gods. Therefore, their alternate descriptions of christology and the Trinity were first and foremost meant to preserve the oneness of God. Ironically, though, the two forms of monarchianism led to opposite conclusions about the person of Christ and his relationship to the Father.

Adoptionism

On one extreme were those who said that **God is one because Jesus is not God**. In other words, they denied the divinity of Christ in order to preserve the oneness of God. This solution to the problem is not a Trinitarian solution, but a *unitarian* one. In this interpretation, Jesus was understood as a mere man who may have been a prophet and who may have been filled with the Holy Spirit for the time of his ministry, but he was essentially the same as you and me. The only real difference between Jesus and the rest of us was that he was able to be perfectly obedient to God, and as a result, God adopted him as Son. In this way, Jesus was seen as having been elevated to a higher status as a reward for his perfection. But he was not understood to be divine by nature. If he was understood to be divine at all, it was a lesser divinity than the Father and an acquired divinity at that. This interpretation of Christ came to be called *adoptionism.*

Adoptionism (sometimes called *dynamic monarchianism*) is the legacy of those, like the Ebionites, who emphasized the humanity of Christ over against the divinity. In fact, the early Church fathers were convinced that the roots of adoptionism went all the way back to the Judaizers of Paul's letters. For the Adoptionists, Jesus is not the giver of the Holy Spirit, but a receiver of the Spirit. In fact, they would say that Jesus was anointed with the Holy Spirit only temporarily, and that when Jesus cried from the cross, "My God, my God, why have you forsaken me?" (Matthew 27:46, Mark 15:34), this was the point at which the Holy Spirit left him to die alone as a mere man. Thus the resurrection of Jesus would have been seen as nothing more than a metaphor for eternal life. The practical result of this was ultimately a rejection of the worship of Christ, and we know of at least one bishop (Paul of Samosata) who tried to discontinue the singing of hymns to Christ in his see (Antioch).

Most Adoptionists also denied the preexistence of Christ, although it became increasingly difficult for them to discount John 1:1, so that over time they speculated that perhaps God had created the Christ spirit before the rest of creation, and that in God's divine foreknowledge of Jesus' perfect obedience, the Christ-spirit was destined to be united with Jesus when the time came for his adoption. They believed this adoption happened at the baptism of Jesus, when the Father was heard to say that he is the beloved Son—as though he had not been the Son until that moment. The phrase *dynamic monarchianism* is a reference to the Greek work *dunamis*, which means "power." The point is that in the adoptionist view, Jesus does not have his own divine power. Any power he had was acquired and received at his baptism.

It is important to note the role that adoption played in the culture of the time. In Roman society, an adult man could be adopted by another in order to pass on an inheritance or to secure the succession of an emperor. No doubt this way of looking at adoption influenced some alternative christologies which saw the relationship between the Father and the Son in terms of the conferral of power from one man to another who was not a blood relative. Adoptionism, therefore, assumed that the Son was not of the same divine nature as the Father, and that the Son did not have any divine power of his own but only received power from God through the indwelling of the Holy Spirit or the Christ-spirit. For the Adoptionists, Jesus was the Son of God, but only by adoption and only after his baptism.

Modalism

At the other extreme were those who attempted to preserve the oneness of God by speculating that there was no distinction between the Father and the Son. In other words, **God is one because Jesus is the Father.** They taught that during his life and ministry, he was "disguised" as a human, but he was not really a human at all, he was simply the Father wearing a human mask. This came to be called *modalism* because the three persons of the Trinity were understood to be only three different "modes" of expression, or functions of the one divine person. Modalists would not speak of three persons, rather they would describe God as one divine person who appeared to humans in three different ways—as if God simply changed hats depending on the task at hand. When he wanted to be the Creator, he put on the Father hat; when he wanted to be the Savior, he put on the Jesus hat; and when he wanted to be the Sanctifier, he put on the Holy Spirit hat. But this meant that Jesus could not really be a human being, since "Jesus" was nothing more than another name for the Father. For the Modalists, the Father and Son are not only *one*, they are one and the same.

Modalism (sometimes called *modalistic monarchianism*) is the opposite of adoptionism, since whereas the Adoptionists affirmed the humanity of Christ but denied his true divinity, the Modalists affirmed his divinity but denied his true humanity. For the Modalists, God is not really understood as "three in one" so much as "one with three names." However, this created a problem that the mainstream theologians were quick to point out: if the Son is the Father incarnate, then the Father died on the cross (a concept that came to be called *patripassionism*, the suffering of the Father). As we have seen, it was understood that the Divine cannot suffer, so to put the Father on the cross would seem to undermine the very divinity of the Father, not to mention imply the death of God. The Modalists apparently countered this argument by affirming a docetic view of Christ which denied any real suffering, and in the process also denied any real human nature. For them, the passion of Christ, as well as his very humanity, were an illusion.

For modalism, the distinctions between the three persons of the Trinity were distinctions in name only, more perceived than real, and entirely from our perspective—not real relationships within a Trinity. We might call God a certain name when we perceive he is doing one thing and call him another name when we perceive he is doing something else, but in the end these names are only functional and have little or nothing to do with God's nature. To look at it another way, God could only be called by one name at a time, and some Modalists even went so far as to say that God should only be called Father in the Old Testament, Son in the New Testament, and Spirit in the Church, as if the functional distinction is also a chronological one. It is easy to see that the Modalists were emphasizing the oneness of God to protect monotheism, however this interpretation had the side effect of removing the human nature from Christ and thereby leaving humanity with no representative, and no real connection to the Divine.

To summarize, the Adoptionists understood a separation between Father and Son that made the Son, not Creator but created. From the perspective of the mainstream bishops, this understanding of the Trinity had too much distinction between Father and Son (to the point of separation) and not enough unity between Father and Son. On the other side, modalism had too much unity and not enough distinction (to the point where Father and Son are thought to be one and the same).

THE MIDDLE WAY

While second-century orthodoxy had been concerned with affirming both the humanity and divinity of Christ, answering the alternative christologies that diminished one or the other, the third century saw the argument develop to include more specific attention to the place of Christ relative to God as Trinity. In the face of new (or more advanced) alternatives, the Church still had to define how it was that Christ could be considered God, without implying that there were two (or three) Gods. As the mainstream Church defined orthodoxy in the face of third-century heresies, it was quite literally defining Christianity itself, or at least the boundaries of what one could believe and still call oneself Christian.

Most bishops and theologians found the truth to be in the middle between the two extremes of adoptionism and modalism. The third-century theologian Novatian would say that Christ was being crucified again between the two thieves of these extreme alternatives. On the one side, the "thief" of adoptionism was trying to steal Christ's divinity, while on the other side, the "thief" of modalism was trying to steal his humanity. Novatian said that the real Christ is the one in the middle between the two false christs. The true Christ is the one who is both divine and human. The mainstream Church argued against adoptionism by asking how a mere human could be the savior of the whole human race. And what of Scriptures that showed Jesus in a unique relationship with God (John 10:30, 14:6)? For that matter, wouldn't Jesus' own claims to that unique relationship disqualify him as a great man or prophet if those claims were not true? Similarly, the Church argued against modalism by asking how one who was not human could give his life as a representative for humanity. And if Jesus only seemed to be human, why did he eat? Furthermore, if Jesus Christ was no more or less than God the Father wearing a human disguise, doesn't that mean that the Father died on the cross?

What was defined as orthodoxy (correct belief) was the middle way between these extreme views. Against the adoptionist interpretation, the Church emphasized Christ's full divinity (Colossians 2:9). Against the modalist interpretation, the Church emphasized that while the Son is divine, he is not the Father (after all, he prayed to the Father).

What is at issue here in finding the orthodox middle is a balance of two important pairs of concepts. The second century had already clarified the first one, which is the affirmation of both natures: humanity and divinity within the person of Christ. This is not a question of either/or, and it is also not a question of 50/50. Though it is paradoxical, we as Christians believe that Jesus Christ was (and is) both fully human and fully divine. The scale cannot tip to either side—he is not more human than divine, nor more divine than human. He is the perfect balance of the fullness of both. The second pair of concepts to be balanced was the unity and distinction within the Trinity. In other words, the Father and Son (and as would later be clarified, the Holy Spirit as well) are one, but not the same; distinct, but not separate.

In response to modalism, the mainstream Church would say that one cannot describe the three persons of the Trinity in terms of mode, function, or activity. In other words, we cannot differentiate between the Father and Son by saying that the Father is Creator and the Son is Redeemer. This is because, as we have already noted, the Son is also Creator (John 1:3) and the Father is also Savior (Exodus 15, Isaiah 63:16). To ascribe different job descriptions to the Father, Son, and Holy Spirit would be to violate the principle of inseparable operation. In fact, the persons of the Trinity are so unified that anything that can be said about one person of the Trinity can be said about the other two as well, a concept called *appropriation* (there are a few exceptions to this, which we will look at later).

Therefore, orthodox theology is the middle way between the extreme alternatives (heresies). As such, it is also the expression of the majority of the Church (guided by the Trinity). It is also the perspective that stands the tests of time and use in the liturgical expression of the community of believers.

Tertullian

Around the turn of the third century, a theologian named Tertullian was the first to clearly define the terminology that the western Church would use to talk about the Trinity. In fact, you may remember that "Trinity" is not in the Bible. It was Tertullian who coined the term (in Latin: *Trinitas*). Tertullian is called the father of Latin theology because of this, and because he pioneered the use of certain Latin terms to explain the Trinity. For example, to explain the three distinct manifestations of God, Tertullian used the word *persona*, or "person." There are three "persons" (*personae*) of the Trinity: Father, Son, and Holy Spirit. To explain the unity, or oneness, of God, Tertullian used the Latin word *substantia*, or "substance." But this does not mean physical or tangible substance, as it might imply when we hear the word in English. It actually means something more like "essence." In other words, the essence of the Trinity is divinity itself, and that essence (or substance) is one divinity shared by all three persons of the Trinity. Put another way, the Trinity is three distinct divine persons who share one substance, and that substance is divinity. It is important to clarify that by using the word "share" to describe the ownership of the divine substance by the three divine persons, I do not mean to imply the kind of sharing that divides. The divine substance is not divided among the three persons (as if each person were one-third of the divinity), rather the term "sharing" as I use it here is meant to emphasize the unity—that it is one divine substance owned by all three persons, and each person is full divinity (*CCC* 253).

If one should ask what we mean by divinity, it is the quality of being divine, which is usually defined in terms of what we might call divine attributes. In other words, to be divine means to be omnipresent (everywhere at all times), omnipotent (all-powerful), and omniscient (all-knowing). We could also add that we assume God is omnibenevolent (always good). Therefore, to say that God is the Supreme Being is to say that he has (and is the only being who has) these attributes. And when Tertullian says that the three persons of the Trinity share one divine substance, it is the "joint ownership" of the one and only divinity that makes the three persons one, and that preserves monotheism for a Church that worships Jesus along with the Father. In other words, we as Christians can say that we believe in one God because there is only one divinity, even though it is shared by the three persons of the Trinity.

Novatian

In the middle of the third century, a Roman priest named Novatian wrote a treatise on the Trinity that took the development of orthodox theology to the next level. For Novatian, as for his predecessors, understanding the Trinity required a correct understanding of christology. And the key to understanding christology was to be found in one of the pre-Pauline hymn texts, Philippians 2:6–11. As we have seen, this passage was probably an early Christian hymn, which Paul quoted to support his exhortation on humility. In this very early christological statement, it is said that in order for Christ to become human, he had to empty himself. This emptying is called *kenosis*, from the Greek term in the text. Novatian used this passage to support his argument for the divinity of Christ, saying that if he had to empty himself to become human, then he must have been more than human to begin with. But for Novatian, this was not enough. To him, the whole thing begged the question—emptied himself of what? To answer that question, Novatian said that Christ had emptied himself of his divine powers—the same things we think of as the divine attributes of omnipresence, omnipotence and omniscience. This does not mean that Christ stopped being divine or became any less divine (he did *not* empty himself of divinity), but it does mean that in order to experience full humanity, Christ voluntarily and temporarily chose not to exercise these divine attributes. Since Jesus the man had to be localized in time and space during his life and ministry on earth, he could not at the same time be omnipresent. Also, in order for him to be able to experience the weakness of the human condition, and especially to suffer and give his life, he could not exercise his omnipotence. Finally, there are a few things Jesus did not know (Matthew 24:36, see Luke 2:52), so he must not have accessed his omniscience in his earthly life. It follows, then, that whatever miracles or other extraordinary acts Jesus performed in his ministry were not done by his own access to divine power, but by the power of the Holy Spirit within him (Matthew 12:28). As we have seen, this is why he could say to his disciples that they could do the same works he did, and even greater works, because they would have access to the same Holy Spirit (John 14:12).

The kenosis (emptying) of Christ is referred to as the christology of descent, meaning that Jesus started out as divine and "descended" to become human (Philippians 2:6–8, John 1:14). This concept will find its way into the Creed, which says, "...for our salvation he came down from heaven." Equally important, Novatian was the first theologian to articulate the fact that the generation, or "begetting," of Christ was not an event that occurred but an eternal state of being. This concept would come to be called eternal generation, and it means that even though the existence of the Son is dependent on the Father, the Son is no less divine and no less eternal than the Father. This concept will also find its way into the Creed, as we will see below.

Novatian was the acting bishop of Rome for about a year and a half in the mid-third century, during a time when the pope had been martyred and persecution prevented the election of a successor. Unfortunately, years after writing his treatise on the Trinity, Novatian would be at the center of a major schism over issues related to penance and reconciliation. He would eventually be raised up as a rival bishop of Rome against the legitimate Pope Cornelius. Thus history has labeled Novatian an "anti-pope." Nevertheless, his contribution to theology and doctrine should not be overlooked. His document on the Trinity is thoroughly orthodox and would even influence later orthodoxy, including the writings of Saints Athanasius and Augustine.

Unity in the Trinity

As I have indicated, it was extremely important to be able to explain the Christian understanding of God in a way that did not imply that Jesus Christ was being worshiped as a second God or as a lesser god. In fact, the major heresies of the early Church were in large part an attempt to correct what the fringe groups perceived as the mainstream Church's mistake: the conviction that God was to be understood as a Trinity of persons. However, for the orthodox bishops, it was the very concept of the Trinity that ensured that God was to be understood as one. It was the single substance of divinity that demonstrated the unity of God.

Just as the very definition of divinity required that God must be immutable and impassible, God must also be simplex, or noncomposite. This means that God cannot be thought of as comprising "parts" or components that make up a whole. This is because, philosophically speaking, anything that has parts can be disassembled, or broken down into its parts. In other words, if God were not simplex—if God were made up of parts—then God could theoretically fall apart, or be broken down into his constituent pieces. Of course this would be unacceptable as a description of God. Another way to say this is that God is incorruptible. It would be assumed that whatever is susceptible to corruption is also susceptible to death, so God is incorruptible because God cannot die. Thus, in order for God to be thought of as eternal, God must be incorruptible, and so God must be simplex. The eternality of God logically requires divine simplicity.

Therefore, while it is true that each of the three persons of the Trinity is not all there is to the Trinity, it cannot be said that God has three parts. Each person of the Trinity is not "part of" God (certainly not one-third of God), since each person of the Trinity must be understood as being fully divine. Although Tertullian did, on occasion, speak of the Son as being "part of" God, later theologians would clarify that this way of speaking of the persons of the Trinity is problematic. In fact, Saint Augustine would insist that not even the mind or will of God are distinct from God's substance. For Augustine, God does not have attributes, since that would imply that the attributes of God are something distinct from God himself. In fact, God does not have anything—God simply is what God is. Rather, what we think of as God's attributes are simply descriptions of the divine substance or of the activity of God.

All this is to say that the unity of the three divine persons in the one divine substance is essential for understanding the nature of God as Trinity. God must be one, and even though we understand God as a perfect balance of oneness and three-ness, nevertheless there is a certain priority of the oneness over the threeness, such that (as Tertullian said) the threeness exists within the oneness. One could say that the threeness exists under the umbrella of oneness.

Hierarchy in the Trinity

On the other hand, the early theologians agreed that some hierarchy was necessary in the Trinity in order to preserve the distinction between persons. In other words, if the Son is not simply the Father in disguise (as the Modalists claimed), then what is the distinction between them? This distinction was described in terms of a hierarchy. The early Church fathers acknowledged that the Father alone was the First Cause, and only the Father is the original and ultimate Source of all things. However, they called the Son the "Second Cause," since he was the agent of creation, through whom all things were made, and through whom all things will be reconciled to their Creator. Even before Tertullian had coined the term "Trinity," the apologists of the second century referred to God as a divine "Triad" in which the Father held the first place, the Son held the second place, and the Holy Spirit held the third place.

However, it is very important to be clear that this hierarchy does not imply that the Son or the Spirit are of a lesser divinity than the Father. Tertullian and Novatian, each in his own way, pointed out that the hierarchy is one of authority, not divinity (or substance). We have already seen this hierarchy of authority described in terms of sender and messenger. In reality, the Son is lower in authority only in relation to the Father. To us the Son is the same authority as the Father, because he comes to us with the Father's authority (Matthew 21:33–46). But this does not mean that the hierarchy only exists from our perspective—to say that would be to describe a form of modalism. It is a real, eternal hierarchy, but one that does not diminish the unity. The terms of distinction in the Trinity are relational (as opposed to functional *CCC* 252, 255), but the distinctions do extend beyond the time of the Incarnation. The distinction of persons in the Trinity must be eternal, otherwise the Trinity would change over time and God would be mutable. The point is that in the Trinity, there is an eternal equality of divinity and eternity (all three persons are co-eternal), but also an eternal hierarchy of authority.

The Church fathers referred to the hierarchy as the *economy*. Today this word means various things, however it is often used to refer to the way humans know God, by his works (*CCC* 236). The phrase "economic Trinity" is used as a reference to God's works *ad extra*—external to the Trinity. However, there is both an external and an internal aspect to the hierarchy in the Trinity. Externally, only the Son is incarnate, and in the Incarnation, he voluntarily takes a subordinate position to do the will of the Father as the Father's messenger. Internally, the economy is in the relationships between the three persons. Just as the Father is not the Son, and the Son is not the Father, so also the Father is not the Father of the Spirit, and the Son is not the Son of the Spirit. The Father is the Father of the Son (and our Father by adoption), but the Father cannot be said to be the Father of the Spirit, since that would imply that the Son and Spirit are "siblings." Likewise, the Son is the Son of the Father, but the Son cannot be said to be the Son of the Spirit, since that would imply that the Father and the Spirit are somehow the "parents" of the Son. Therefore, even though these relational terms are primarily for our understanding, they are important, because they do describe something of the nature of the internal relationships of the Trinity.

BAPTISM IN THE NAME OF THE TRINITY

The doctrine of the Trinity is the one thing on which all Christians should agree, because it is in this understanding of God that we find the very definition of Christianity. In other words, one who does not accept the doctrine of the Trinity should not presume to call himself or herself a Christian. This is what the Apostle Paul meant by one faith and one baptism (Ephesians 4:4–6). Paul affirms that there is only one body of Christ, and only one baptism into that one body, and although we are divided by denominations today, baptism by any one denomination should be considered valid in any other denomination, as long as it is done in the name of the Father, Son, and Holy Spirit (technically speaking, a valid baptism also requires the element of baptism, water, and requires that the person conducting the baptism "have the intention of doing that which the Church does" [*CCC* 1284]).

The Church councils of the third and fourth centuries confirmed that what makes a baptism valid is the invocation of the name of the Trinity. Thus the Church has affirmed that God is at work in every baptism, as long as the name of the Trinity is used. However, some denominations promote an alternate view of baptism that makes the validity of the baptism dependent on the age of the one being baptized. These groups routinely rebaptize anyone who wants to join their community especially those baptized as infants. The Council of Arles in 314 CE condemned rebaptism as heretical and schismatic. One of the canons of the council stated, "...If anyone comes to the Church from a heresy, let them ask him the Creed, and if it shall appear certain that he was baptized in the Father and the Son and the Holy Spirit, let him receive only the laying on of hands [confirmation], that he may receive the Holy Spirit. But if, when he is asked, his reply does not contain this Trinity, let him be baptized" (Council of Arles, Canon 8). Later this was also confirmed at the Council of Nicaea in 325. Of course, the faith of the one receiving baptism must be sincere, but from the earliest days of the Church there was no age limit; it was assumed that "household" faith (that is, the faith of the parents) could suffice for one too young to be accountable for his or her own faith (see Acts 11:14, Acts 16:15, and 1 Corinthians 1:16, 7:14).

Therefore, a denomination or group that rebaptizes is guilty of dividing the body (1 Corinthians 12:12–25, see also Ephesians 4:1–6). If a person was baptized in the name of the Trinity, no matter the age or denomination, that baptism is valid, and to baptize that person again at a later time constitutes rebaptism, which is an act of schism against the one body of Christ, and which denies the activity and sovereignty of God in the sacrament. If the baptism of a heretic returning to the Church does not need to be repeated, then certainly the baptism of one who was innocent also does not need to be repeated.

This begs the question, if the only thing required for a valid baptism is that it is done in the name of the Trinity, what would make a baptism invalid? If a valid baptism is one that is conducted in the name of the Father, Son, and Holy Spirit, as directed by Jesus (Matthew 28:19), it follows that a baptism in any other name is not a Christian baptism. Baptisms that use alternative formulas are invalid because they violate doctrines associated with the Trinity and teach (or imply) a false understanding of the Trinity. The most common example of this is a trend to recast the Trinitarian formula in terms such as "Creator, Redeemer, Sustainer," or something similar. Such a change is often justified as an attempt to remove a perceived masculine bias in the words "Father" and "Son." However, as we have seen, to describe the persons of the Trinity in terms of function is actually a form of modalism, because it compromises inseparable operation by implying that the Father is not also Savior and Sustainer, or that the Son is not also Creator and Sanctifier.

Therefore, while there is nothing wrong with speaking of the persons of the Trinity in terms of divine activity (for example when the Holy Spirit is said to inspire the writing of Scripture), the biblical Trinitarian formula must always be used (especially in the sacraments) and we must be careful to be clear that in reality it is the Trinity who created the universe, inspired the prophets and apostles, and who reaches out to humanity in reconciliation.

SUMMARY

From the very beginning of the Church's existence, the conviction that it was not only appropriate but in fact mandatory to worship Christ forced the early Christians to have to answer the problem of Trinitarian monotheism. The worship of Christ was at the heart of the issue because some were arguing that a mere human should not be worshiped (Ebionites and Adoptionists), while others were arguing that one who is worthy of worship should not be said to have suffered and died (gnostics and some Modalists). To the first group, the obvious humanity of Jesus seemed to negate his divinity, since it was assumed that divinity requires immutability and impassibility. To the second group, the assumed divinity of Christ seemed to negate his full humanity. And although the Church quickly clarified that it was not his divine nature that suffered, this only began to answer the question.

Eventually, the emergence of alternative answers to the

question of Christian monotheism forced the mainstream Church to refine its own answers, and orthodoxy gained increasing clarity. The process of the development of doctrine can be described using the three laws:

1. Heresy forces orthodoxy to define itself.
2. Orthodoxy is the middle way between the extreme alternatives.
3. Christology informs soteriology.

The point at issue ultimately becomes one of soteriology, which for the moment can be thought of in terms of the connection (or reconciliation) between God and humanity. The docetic/gnostic/modalist interpretation of Christ has a connection to the Divine, in one form or another, but lacks a true connection to humanity, and so this understanding is that of a Christ who cannot represent humanity to God. The Ebionite/adoptionist interpretation is of a Christ who is part of humanity, but who lacks any real (ontological) connection to the Divine, and so cannot represent God to humanity in a way that would constitute true divine intervention in the world. In either case, salvation must be understood as something other than atonement, as it is reduced to the Savior simply "showing the way," either by setting an example or bringing knowledge.

For the Adoptionists, God is one because Jesus is not God. For the Modalists, God is one because Jesus is the Father. Both of these extremes were determined to be inadequate as a description of God. Orthodoxy is then defined as the middle way between the extreme alternatives—it is that interpretation of Christ and the Trinity which is consistent with the whole witness of Scripture and previous tradition. Orthodoxy affirms that the Father and Son are one (John 10:30), but not one and the same (John 14:28). Jesus is God, but not the Father.

We noted that both extremes of adoptionism and modalism rejected the concept of a bodily resurrection of Jesus

Christ. Adoptionists would have interpreted the resurrection as nothing more than a metaphor for eternal life. Modalists would have interpreted the resurrection as a docetic vision of a less-than-human Jesus. Against both extremes, orthodoxy affirms the real bodily resurrection of Jesus.

The two most important proponents of orthodoxy in the third century were Tertullian and Novatian, and in fact it could be said that they defined orthodoxy for their time and beyond. Tertullian coined the term *Trinity* and gave the Church the terms *substance* and *persons* to describe the oneness and threeness of the Trinity. Although he was not the first to say it, Tertullian solidified the definition of the oneness of God in terms of the one divine substance. Novatian described the Incarnation in terms of the *kenosis*, solidifying the Church's understanding of the christology of descent. He was also the pioneer of the doctrine of eternal generation, which is an outgrowth of Tertullian's concept of the single substance, and which affirms that the single divinity also implies an equal eternity of the Father and Son (and Spirit).

Therefore, the conclusions of the orthodox theologians demonstrated that the Trinity is to be understood in terms of a balance of unity and distinction. The unity is found in the single divine substance, the singular power and activity (inseparable operation), and the equal eternity of the three persons. This unity is based on the assumptions of divine simplicity, immutability, impassibility, and incorruptibility. Inseparable operation also leads to the doctrine of appropriation, which affirms that anything one can say about any one person of the Trinity can also be said about the other two persons and vice versa. There are only a few exceptions to the doctrine of appropriation (which will be discussed below), and these exceptions are precisely related to the distinction of persons within the Trinity. The distinction is found in the hierarchy of authority, and in the fact that only the Son was incarnate. However, we must always maintain that the hierarchy of the Trinity is not an ontological hierarchy—it is not a hierarchy of divinity—it is a hierarchy of authority, and even then the equal divinity of the Son demands that any submission we ascribe to him must be voluntary.

DISCUSSION QUESTIONS

1. Why might the concept of "Christian monotheism" have sounded like a contradiction in the time of the first Christians?

2. How would the early Christians have answered the charge that being crucified would disqualify Jesus as the Messiah? How did the Apostle Paul answer it (see Galatians 3:13)?

3. What did it mean for the early Christians to worship Christ, and what implications did that have for Christian theology?

4. What is orthodoxy, and how can it be said that orthodoxy has always existed in every generation of the Church?

5. What is heresy, and why couldn't the Church let people believe whatever they wish?

6. In what ways is the orthodox understanding of the Christ and the Trinity the middle way between the two extremes of adoptionism and modalism?

7. What was the theologian Tertullian's contribution to our understanding of the Trinity?

8. What is the doctrine of "eternal generation"?

9. How do we understand the unity of the three persons of the Trinity in such a way that it preserves the oneness of God?

10. How do we understand the distinction between the three persons of the Trinity so we avoid the heresy of modalism? How is recasting the Trinitarian formula as "Creator, Redeemer, Sustainer" a form of modalism, and why is that a problem?

CHAPTER 3

The Nicene Creed

Arianism—
Diminishing the Divinity of the Son

In the early fourth century, a priest in the city of Alexandria began preaching a form of adoptionism. His name was Arius, and the scandal that was created by his teaching came to be known as the Arian controversy (this has nothing to do with the so-called "Aryan race"; the similarity of names is purely coincidental). Although Arius did accept the idea of the preexistence of Christ (from John 1:1), he taught that Christ was not eternally preexistent, but that he was a created being. According to Arius, the Father created the Son at some point before the creation of the rest of the universe. This meant that, for Arius, the Son is not eternal as the Father is, because there was a span of time before the creation of the Son. Arius was famous for saying, "There was a time when he was not," meaning that he believed there was a time when the Son did not exist. He argued that if the Father and the Son were both divine by nature and both eternal, then that would imply that they are two Gods. Arius said that if the Son is eternal, then the Father and Son are really "brothers."

True to his adoptionist roots, Arius believed that Jesus was not divine by nature, but that he was a mere human who achieved perfect obedience to God and was rewarded with an elevated status, which for Arius was a quasi-divinity. Arius taught that since God foreknew the perfect obedience of the man Jesus, he created the Christ (or *Logos*) before the creation of the world and predestined the Christ to indwell the man Jesus at the time of his adoption (his baptism). Therefore Jesus was adopted by God just as we might be, which means that he doesn't so much save humanity as show us the way to salvation. If we are to be saved, it would be by following his example and, through our own obedience, gaining adoption for ourselves. In contrast to the christology of descent of Tertullian and Novatian, Arius' christology is a *christology of ascent*: For Arius, Jesus is not God who became human (as in John 1:14), Jesus is a man who became a god.

While the orthodox bishops maintained that the hierarchy of the Trinity was a hierarchy of authority, but not of divinity, Arius was teaching a hierarchy of divinity. Whatever divinity he believed Jesus had was an acquired divinity (not by nature) and a lesser divinity than the Father. It seems that Arius' understanding of the Word was more like Philo's *logos* than John's. The orthodox bishops, on the other hand, would not accept the idea of degrees of divinity. One is either fully divine by nature or not at all. For the orthodox, the unity of the Trinity is in the one substance of divinity, and the distinction is in the hierarchy of authority. For Arius, the only unity is in the cooperation of the Son's will with the Father—everything else is distinction, to the point of separation. He believed that the Father and Son are not only distinct, they are separate, because the Son is created.

After he was confronted by his bishop, Alexander of Alexandria, Arius accused the bishop of the heresy of modalism (the opposite extreme from his own heresy), and the controversy that followed threatened to split the Church in the east.

Athanasius of Alexandria

The orthodox response to Arius was articulated best by Athanasius, who eventually became bishop of Alexandria after Alexander. Athanasius, building on the work of Tertullian and Novatian, clarified that while the Son was begotten from the Father (meaning that the Son's existence is caused by, or contingent on, the Father), the Son was not created. In fact the Son is eternal and has always existed with the Father. If this were not so, then the Father would not always have been a Father, since there would have been a time before the begetting of the Son. Borrowing from Novatian, Athanasius countered Arius' "There was a time when he was not" with a slogan of his own: "Always a Father, always a Son." In other words, God has always been a Trinity. This is, of course, required by the doctrine of divine immutability—God cannot change, and so the first person of the Trinity cannot go from not being a Father to being a Father. Following John 1:1–5, 10–14, Athanasius emphasized that while we may hope to be adopted sons and daughters of God, Jesus Christ is in fact the only "natural" Son of God.

Against the adoptionist reluctance to worship Jesus, Athanasius would later compare Jesus Christ to the images of the emperor that were worshiped in the time of the early Church. Just as worshiping the image of the emperor is the same as worshiping the emperor, so worshiping Jesus Christ, the image of the Father, is the same as worshiping the Father. And yet, no one would assume that the image of the emperor is the emperor himself, so we also make a distinction between the Son and the Father. Thus we see that the unity of the Father and Son allows us to worship the Son (against adoptionism), while at the same time the distinction prevents us from thinking that the Father and the Son are one and the same (against modalism).

Superman Versus Batman

If we may borrow an analogy from popular culture, a good way to think about this is to consider the difference between Superman and Batman. Superman is a "strange visitor from another planet" who *comes down* to earth to be a powerful savior of the human race. He is more than human but comes to live with us, becoming one of us, in order to save us. Batman is a mere (flawed) man who, through self-sacrifice, personal discipline, and in short, willpower, strives to become a hero. He has no superhuman powers, but he does heroic things—things anyone could do with the proper fortitude—but more important he sets an example of resistance against evil. However, in the end he is really just a vigilante who is seen by some as a positive role model. In this analogy, Superman represents the christology of descent (orthodoxy) and Batman represents the christology of ascent (the heresy of adoptionism). The point is that salvation requires more than willpower, it requires divine intervention, which is why the bishops of the early Church concluded that a christology of ascent would be inadequate for salvation.

Many modern hero stories are variations on the Christ story. Some of them may even be unintentionally copying the most compelling elements of the story, such as self sacrifice ("no one has greater love than this, to lay down one's life for one's friends," John 15:13) and resurrection. However, most superhero stories in popular culture actually present more of an Arian picture of their Christ figure than an orthodox one. In other words, most movies present the hero more as the result of human striving than divine intervention. One notable exception is Luc Besson's 1997 film *The Fifth Element*. The Christ figure, "Leeloo," played by Milla Jovovich, is the "supreme being" who comes down to earth to be the savior of the human race. There is even an Incarnation scene, in which she is reconstructed from a few cells using her DNA. Finally, she cannot save humanity without some human response, which comes from the film's Everyman, played by Bruce Willis. Although this sci-fi cult classic may seem like a strange example of the Christ story, it is one of the few depictions of a christology of descent, with "divine intervention" taking the initiative, and the human participation as a response to the Divine. And although this film may seem obscure (and not suitable for all ages), its obscurity underscores the relative rarity of hero stories that portray anything like the orthodox christology of descent.

For some reason, human nature loves to identify with the Arian Christ—the flawed hero who pulls himself up by his own boot straps and *achieves* hero status through personal growth. Of course there is nothing wrong with this in fiction, and it can provide a good moral example for us to follow. But it is ironic, because while people want a more accessible hero (one who makes it OK to be flawed), they end up with a picture of a version of salvation that is based on human effort. In the movies, the hero's action can save others without divine intervention, but in the atonement, if the hero is a mere human, then he cannot even save himself, let alone others. Perhaps this attraction to the self-made hero is why Arius' interpretation of Christ became so popular in the fourth century. No doubt it also caught on because of the adoptionist desire to "protect" the oneness of God by removing Jesus from the realm of the divine.

In any case, the bishops of the fourth century recognized that the difference between the christology of descent and the christology of ascent is in the soteriology. Remember law number three, *christology informs soteriology*—what we believe about Christ (christology) has a direct impact on what we believe about salvation (soteriology). If we believe in a christology of descent, then salvation happens by divine intervention. The Word becomes human and lives with us, and dies for us. But if we believe in a christology of ascent, then "salvation" is really nothing more than a good example for us to follow, and in the end we must save ourselves. So part of the reason that the christology of ascent was ultimately rejected by the early Church was that the form of salvation that it implies would leave Christians in despair, wondering if any could follow the example well enough to earn a place in heaven.

In the year 325 CE, a worldwide council of bishops was held in the city of Nicaea, in what is now Turkey. The council was held to discuss several issues in the Church, but the most important was the Arian controversy. The main result of the council was the writing of a Creed. This Creed was expanded at another council in the city of Constantinople in 381 CE, and would become what we now know as the Nicene Creed. The Creed is not only a statement of faith (the word "creed" is from the Latin *credo*, which means "I believe"), it is in many ways a summary of Christian doctrine, as it has come to us from sacred Scripture and tradition. Much like the Ten Commandments are a summary of the Old Testament, the Nicene Creed is a summary of the New Testament: It helps us interpret it and understand it. The Creeds of the Church are an important part of the Church's tradition because they set the standard for the interpretation of Scripture. Scripture alone is not enough without the Creeds (*CCC* 81–82). This is proven by the fact that the heretics were getting their alternative interpretations from the same Scriptures.

PNEUMATOMACHIANISM— DIMINISHING THE DIVINITY OF THE HOLY SPIRIT

Tertullian and Novatian had both affirmed the divine personhood of the Holy Spirit. However, after the Council of Nicaea, some of the Arians (and some of the various factions known as "Semi-Arians") eventually accepted the divinity of the Son but were reluctant to accept the divinity of the Spirit. They apparently used the same arguments that Arius had used against the divinity of the Son, but now against the divinity of the Holy Spirit. These people came to be called *pneumatomachians*, which means, those who fight against the Spirit. They were also called Macedonians, after one of their early leaders. Athanasius wrote against them, as did a group of bishops known as the *Cappadocian fathers*: Basil of Caesarea, Gregory of Nyssa, and Gregory of Nazianzus. Thanks to the Cappadocians, the full personhood and divinity of the Holy Spirit was clarified for the eastern church at the Council of Constantinople in 381 CE. There the bishops affirmed that the Holy Spirit is to be understood as equal in divinity and eternity with the Father just as the Son is, and therefore it is appropriate to worship the Holy Spirit as well.

THE NICENE CREED

The Creed we know as the Nicene Creed was mostly produced by the Council of Nicaea in 325 CE, but later expanded (especially the paragraph on the Spirit) at the Council of Constantinople in 381 CE. Virtually every line in the Creed was put there specifically to exclude the alternative christologies, especially the Arian version of adoptionism. Therefore, the Creed became a summary of the orthodox interpretation of the Scriptures concerning the Trinity, endorsed by a worldwide council of bishops (in reality most of the bishops were from the east). When one examines the Creed, one notices that it is written in a Trinitarian outline, since it was created using a baptismal statement of faith based on Matthew 28:19. Also, it is important to note that there is very little in the Creed that is new. It was based on all of the concepts that we have covered so far in this book. The Nicene Creed affirms the full humanity and full divinity of Jesus Christ, the second person of the Trinity. It affirms the christology of descent, that Jesus is the Word made flesh (John 1:14). It affirms that God has always been a Trinity and that there was never a time when the Son of God did not exist. It affirms that Jesus Christ and the Holy Spirit share the same divine essence as God the Father, and so it is appropriate to worship Christ and the Holy Spirit, for when one worships the Son of God or the Spirit of God, one is worshiping God.

Let's take a look at the Creed line by line to examine the significance of each part. I encourage you to think about the meaning of each sentence in the Creed, so that when you say it in worship, you will not be saying the words only, but you will be thinking about the meaning behind those words.

I believe in one God, the Father almighty

The Creed begins with the conviction that there is only one God. Whatever we go on to say we believe, it must fit within the monotheistic framework inherited from Judaism. Although this framework is now modified to include the divinity of Christ and the Holy Spirit, it must be understood in such a way that it does not compromise the oneness of God. It is also important to clarify that the Father whom Jesus taught is one and the same with the God of the Old Testament. The docetics and gnostics would have argued that the God of the Old Testament was a different (and meaner) God than the one whom Jesus came to reveal. They maintained that the God and Father of the Lord Jesus Christ was a higher and more benevolent God than the Creator described in the Old Testament. The Creed therefore excludes these heresies, by affirming the oneness of God and (implying) that the two testaments of the Christian Bible together proclaim the one God.

Notice that God is described as omnipotent (almighty). This is one of the primary divine attributes that we assume defines divinity itself. As Tertullian had pointed out, the fact that God is omnipotent rules out the possibility of any other gods, since a God who is all-powerful leaves no room for the supposed powers of other gods. In other words, polytheism assumes that there are many gods, all with their own powers and spheres of influence. But if that were true, then none of them could be all-powerful, since they would each have to defer to the other gods to a certain extent. Therefore, omnipotence negates the possibility of multiple gods—there cannot be more than one omnipotent being, or omnipotence itself is compromised. Therefore, there is only one divinity and only one divine omnipotence in the Trinity. Here in this line of the Creed, omnipotence is associated with the Father, since the Father is the Source of divine power, but it is the same omnipotence as that of the Son and the Spirit. As Novatian noted, the Son can set aside his prerogative to exercise divine omnipotence, but as later theologians would clarify, it is not really a separate power from that of the Father. The oneness of God means that the Trinity is not three separate divine powers. Therefore the divinity, the divine power, and indeed the very existence, of the Son and Spirit are dependent on, and never separate from, the divinity of the Father.

It is worth noting that it is not a heresy to call the first person of the Trinity "Mother," since the aspects of parenting that we may associate with motherhood are appropriately ascribed to our Creator-Parent (*CCC* 239, see Isaiah 66:13, Psalm 131:2). However the term "Mother" should never be substituted for "Father" in the Trinitarian formula, especially in baptism, since as we have seen, that would invalidate the baptism.

Maker of heaven and earth, of all things visible and invisible

As we noted in chapter one, calling God "Father" is also a way of describing the fact that God is Creator of, and Provider for, all of creation (*CCC* 238–239). The first person of the Trinity is the ultimate Source and origin of all that is, even of the Son and the Spirit (*CCC* 245). Therefore, in addition to affirming that the Father of Jesus Christ is the God of the Old Testament, this line rejects any docetic or gnostic notion that the Creator is a lesser divinity or demi-god. It also rejects the dualism inherent in these heresies which maintained a strict separation between the spiritual and the physical realms. On the contrary, the Creed affirms that both the spiritual and the material are part of the one creation. The material world was created good by the one good God, no less than the spiritual realm. This implies that evil is not part of creation, and so it cannot be blamed on the God of the Old Testament.

I believe in one Lord Jesus Christ, the Only Begotten Son of God

As we saw in 1 Corinthians 8:6, the Father is called the "one God," and the Son is called the "one Lord." The title "Lord" is a testimony to the divinity of Christ, since it is the substitution for the divine name. Therefore, even though the Father and Son are not one and the same, they are unified in divinity. Jesus is the Only Begotten Son of God, which means that he is the Son of God's own nature, and therefore he is unique among humanity. We are also children of God, but by adoption. While he is fully human, he is also fully divine, and as the divine Son of God, he is the only "natural" child of God and the heir of all that belongs to the Father.

To be *begotten* means that the Son's existence has a Source, which is the Father. The Father, as First Cause, has no Source, and is therefore *unbegotten*. The Son is dependent on the Father, but the Father is not dependent on the Son. This concept of "begottenness" can be expressed in more modern English as *generation*. We say that the Son is generated from the Father, and that the Father is ungenerated. The generation of the Son of God encompasses both his unity with the Father, and his distinction from the Father. As the early theologians explained, whatever is generated must be of the same substance as that which generates it. So the Son is of the same divine substance as the Father, the same divinity. On the other hand, whatever is generated must also be distinct from that which generates it. So the Son is distinct from the Father, as the One who is generated (begotten, or caused) is distinct from the One who generates (unbegotten, or the First Cause). Therefore, the generation of the Son is a theological way of saying that the Son is the same Divinity as the Father, but he is not identical with the Father. This is exactly what we read in John 1:1, "the Word was *with* God (distinct from the Father), and the Word *was* God (the same divinity)."

Born of the Father before all ages

The primary point debated at the Council of Nicaea was the question of whether the Son was co-eternal with the Father. Arius had claimed that the Son was created, and that before his creation, he did not exist. The Arians allowed that he may have been the agent of creation, but they argued that he was himself created at some prior point. "There was a time when he was not" was the Arian slogan. But this implied that there was a time when the Father was not a Father, and God was not a Trinity. As Athanasius would reply (borrowing from Novatian), "Always a Father, always a Son." The orthodox bishops argued that Christ did not come into existence, but he was eternal in the past, just as the Father was. There was no time lag before the Son was begotten, for if there were, God would have undergone a change (from not being a Father to being a Father), which would compromise divine immutability and indeed the very definition of divinity.

Therefore, the Creed affirms that there was never a time when Christ did not exist, because he is eternally with God

(John 1:1). Even though he is begotten, and his existence is dependent on the Father, that does not mean that he is created, or that there was a beginning to his existence. Some translations of the Creed say, "eternally begotten of the Father..." which is a reference to the doctrine of eternal generation. The Son is not generated in time (which would imply a beginning to his existence), but he is eternally generated ("before all ages"). Novatian had clarified that the generation of the Son is not an event (not even an event before time), but the generation of the Son is an eternal state being. It is a way of describing the fact that the same divinity of Father and Son also means they share the same eternality.

God from God, Light from Light, true God from true God

The line "true God from true God" was added specifically to refute Arian adoptionism. It affirms that the Son is no less divine than the Father. He is not of a lesser divinity or an acquired divinity. He is fully divine and the same divinity as the Father.

Therefore, these last two sentences together affirm both the eternal generation of the Son as well as the eternal co-existence of the Father and Son. The co-eternality of the Father and Son further demonstrates the divinity of Christ and his eternal equality with the Father. To say that the Son is "God from God, Light from Light, true God from true God" further emphasizes his full and equal divinity. However it also reminds us of the distinction between the Father and the Son. The Father is God; the Son is "God *from* God." The Father is Light; the Son is "Light *from* Light." The divinity is the same, but there is still a distinction. The Father and Son are one, but they are not one and the same. They are unified in divinity and eternality, but they are not identical because of the distinction between the Unbegotten One (First Cause) and the Begotten One.

Begotten, not made, consubstantial with the Father

This line is also meant to be an anti-Arian statement. Christ was not created, not even before the rest of creation. Based on what the third-century theologians had written, the majority of the bishops at Nicaea reasoned that the one who is begotten (the Son) must have the same divine and uncreated nature as the one who begets (the Father). The fact that the Son is begotten of the Father means that the Son's existence is generated from the Father's, but not in the sense that the Father existed first without the Son. Thus the Son is eternally generated, not created at some point before creation.

The word *consubstantial* may be new to some people. Some translations of the Creed have said, "one in being with the Father." But sometimes this has been misunderstood as though it implies that the Father and the Son are one and the same, which is not the case. The phrase "one in being" is an English translation of the Greek word *homoousios* which literally means, *of the same essence*. This is the same as when Tertullian said that the Father and Son (and the Holy Spirit) share the same divine substance. Therefore when the Greek word is translated into English via Latin, it becomes *consubstantial*—same substance. This is related to what we noted above: what is generated must be the same substance as the Source of generation. As a shortcut you can remember that consubstantial means two things: same divinity and same eternity. In other words, the Son is the same divinity as the Father and is also co-eternal with the Father. Because there is only one God, there can be only one divinity, so the divinity of the Son is the divinity of the Father. And since divinity must be eternal, the equal divinity means the Father and Son are also equally eternal in both the past and the future.

This is related to the concept of *divine simplicity*, which says that divinity is indivisible. As I have noted above, God does not have "parts" because anything with parts can be broken down into its parts and thus decay. Thus it is not appropriate to speak of the three persons of the Trinity as three "parts" of God or to say that the Son is "part" of God. It is true that the Son is God and that the Son is not all there is to God, yet to use the word "part" or "parts" would imply that the three persons of the Trinity are each one third of the Divine, which is of course not the case. Each of the three persons of the Trinity is fully God (Divine). Therefore, divine simplicity requires that God be one, and that the Father and Son (and the Spirit) be the same divinity, since any being that is not the same divinity as the Father would not be God at all. So all three persons of the Trinity are the same divine substance. The concept of consubstantiality, then, affirms the ontological (essential) unity between Father and Son while admitting to a certain distinction, since one would not describe a thing as "of the same essence" as itself.

The Greek word *homoousios* (consubstantial) actually caused a bit of a controversy itself when it was used in the Creed. The problem was that the word is not found in Scripture. The Arians argued the word should not be used for that reason, however the majority of the bishops finally accepted the word as the best way to interpret the biblical witness to the Trinity. In the end, it was the only term the bishops of the council could find that would describe the relationship of the Son to the Father without being vague enough also to allow an Arian interpretation. Thus Scripture alone was not enough, since both the Arians and the orthodox were reading the same Scriptures but coming to very different interpretations. In the Creed, then, the bishops implicitly decided that the Church had to go beyond Scripture to interpret Scripture. Therefore, the Creed became part of our tradition, which helps us interpret Scripture.

It is important to note that later Church councils would affirm that the Son (in his human nature) is also consubstantial with humanity. The fact that he is consubstantial with both the Trinity and humanity is what allows him to be the mediator and reconciler of God and humanity. In fact, the doctrine of *communicatio idiomatum* affirms that the union of Christ's divine and human natures allows each nature to communicate, or share, the idiomatic properties of the other nature. This means that by virtue of the union of divine and human in the person of Christ, his divine nature was able to experience the human condition, and his human nature was able to be glorified. And since Christ's human nature is consubstantial with all of humanity, our human nature can be glorified through identification with him. This does not mean that his divine nature suffered, but it does mean that God can understand what it's like to be us. The fact is that the point of contact of the human and divine natures in the person of Christ is the very nexus of communion between humanity and God.

Through him all things were made

Quoting from John 1:3, this line affirms that Christ is the agent of creation. Just as we read in Genesis that God created by his word, John also tells us that it was through the Word of God that all creation came into existence. The Arians would have said that to the Father, the Son is created, but from our perspective, the Son is the agent of creation. This means that the Arians saw Christ, not really as both divine and human, but somewhere in between the divine and the human. Against this, the Creed affirms the Son's full and equal divinity as Creator with the Father.

The orthodox bishops wanted to make a clear distinction between that which is uncreated and that which is created. A being is either Creator or created, there is no in between, and for the majority of the bishops of Nicaea, Jesus Christ is Creator, not created. In fact, based on the doctrine of inseparable operation, it is just as accurate to say that the Son is Creator as it is to say that the Father is Creator, because Father and Son are unified in all divine activity (*CCC* 292). This understanding rules out any modalistic formula for the Trinity that would define the Father as Creator, to the exclusion of the Son.

For us men and for our salvation
he came down from heaven

Here is the christology of descent spelled out in the Creed. Jesus Christ is the eternal Word of God who became flesh (John 1:14). He *came down*—that is, he is God who became human, not a human who became a god (John 6:38). He is the Son and heir of the Father who temporarily set aside (chose not to use) his divine powers (Philippians 2:6–11), and became human in an act of divine intervention, so that salvation could be offered to the human race by God's merciful invitation of forgiveness. The mention of salvation reminds us that *christology informs soteriology* (law number three). The orthodox understanding of salvation is that it requires divine intervention and is not accomplished solely by human effort. The phrase, "for us men" means that the Incarnation was for the sake of all of humanity.

And by the Holy Spirit
was incarnate of the Virgin Mary, and became man

The same Holy Spirit who anointed and inspired the prophets was the agent of the Incarnation (Matthew 1:18, 20, Luke 1:35). This should not be taken too literally, as though the Holy Spirit impregnated Mary. It simply means that it was the power of God present in the Holy Spirit that created the human body of Jesus in the womb of Mary. In reality the whole Trinity effected the Incarnation (by virtue of inseparable operation), but only the first person of the Trinity is to be called the Father of Jesus. What is more important to note is that the divine Word of God voluntarily set aside his omnipresence in order to enter Mary's womb and be born into the world as a human being—for a while not to be everywhere at once, but localized in time and space. Thus even the divine nature of Christ was circumscribed, united with his human nature in Mary's womb, and so (as a later Church council would clarify) Mary gave birth to the whole person of Christ, including his divine nature (Luke 1:43). This is why it is appropriate to call Mary "Mother of God" (in Greek, *Theotokos*).

This is not meant to imply a limitation of the divine nature of Christ that would in any sense diminish his divinity. But it is a beautiful reminder of God's love for humanity that the divine Word was willing to submit to human birth and a life of humility, not to mention death on a cross. To my mind, the heart of the mystery of the Trinity is how the divinity of Christ is one and the same as the divinity of the Father, and yet the divine nature of Christ is an eternally distinct person, eternally the second person of the Trinity. The divine nature of Jesus was never limited nor diminished, and yet he was circumscribed within the womb of the Virgin.

The phrase, "became man" really means "became truly human," and is an argument against the various forms of gnosticism or modalism that denied the full humanity of Jesus. Although the Gospel of John says the words "became flesh," later councils of the Church would have to clarify that it is not enough to say that he became *flesh*, since that could imply less than a full humanity, as if he were a spirit who only put on a suit of flesh. A bishop named Apollinarius had proposed that perhaps the person of Jesus Christ had no human mind or will, and that the divine *Logos* had replaced the human mind in Jesus. This way of understanding Christ was meant to explain why Jesus did not sin, but it was declared a heresy because it diminished the humanity of Jesus. Without a human mind, he would be less than fully human. Therefore, it is important to clarify that he became *man*, that is, fully human, not just "flesh." It is never appropriate to substitute the word "flesh" at this point in the Creed.

For our sake he was crucified under Pontius Pilate, he suffered death and was buried

This line exists to place the Christ event in history. The story of the passion of Christ is not a myth, nor is it something that is said to have happened before recorded history. It happened in the time of the Roman occupation of Judea, when Pontius Pilate was the Roman officer in charge. This is a historically verifiable situation: Pilate was in office from 26 to 36 CE. During that time, Jesus Christ was perceived as a threat to established order and was executed by crucifixion. His death was "for our sake" because it has significance for our salvation. Jesus died as a representative of humanity, the one perfect human became a substitute for the rest of the human race (Hebrews 10:1–18). By sacrificing his life and voluntarily giving himself up to death, he "paid a price he did not owe, because we owed a price we could not pay," or to paraphrase Saint Paul, he took our curse on himself so that we could receive the blessing that is rightfully his (Galatians 3:13–14).

By emphasizing the fact that Jesus really died, this line also continues the affirmation of his true humanity, against any docetic, gnostic or modalist christology that might deny it. This is also a refutation of modalism (perceived as patripassionism) because it affirms that it was the Son who suffered and died, not the Father. By mentioning the death and burial, this line is also meant to rule out any speculation that Jesus had not really died; that perhaps he was only passed out and was revived later.

And rose again on the third day
in accordance with the Scriptures

Of course, as Christians we believe that Jesus did not stay dead. Having died for our sins, he was vindicated as sinless by the resurrection. This line of the Creed is taken verbatim from 1 Corinthians 15:3–4.

Most of the alternative christologies that existed in the early Church denied the bodily resurrection of Jesus. Those christologies that denied his full humanity (docetism, gnosticism, modalism) also denied a bodily resurrection, since many of them believed he had no real human body. Those who did believe he had a physical body saw the resurrection as a shedding of the body to reveal Christ's true spiritual self. Thus the body was not raised, but the Christ-spirit only, being freed from the prison of the flesh. Ironically, those christologies at the other end of the spectrum that denied the divinity of Christ also did not believe in a bodily resurrection. They taught that the resurrection was only a metaphor for eternal life, and for them, to say that Jesus was raised to life only meant that he went to heaven. Against these, the Creed affirms that Jesus' resurrection was real (as the gospels say it was), and was neither a ghostly apparition nor merely a metaphor for heaven.

He ascended into heaven
and is seated at the right hand of the Father

After a time of post-resurrection ministry, Jesus ascended from his state of humility and reclaimed the divine glory that was originally his from before time (John 17:5, 24, Philippians 2:9–11). The ascension is a restoration to the prior status of the Son, it is not a reward for obedience or for a successful ministry.

The phrase, "at the right hand of the Father" is an image of the shared divine essence and the unity of divine power between the Father and the Son (*CCC* 663). Yet the hierarchy remains in the concept of agency. The Son is at the right hand of the Father and yet it is still the Father's right hand. The image of the "right hand" is a metaphor for power, authority, and agency. The Son exercises the one divine power according to the Father's authority and as the Father's agent—not only agent of creation and agent of redemption but as the agent of judgment as well. The Son has resumed his place of equality (Philippians 2:6) but is still voluntarily subject to the Father's will. This demonstrates that the hierarchy of the Trinity, while voluntary (because of the equal divinity of the three persons) is not simply a function of the Incarnation, nor is it temporary or time-bound. The hierarchy of authority is based on the priority of generation, in other words, that the Unbegotten One is the Source of the Begotten One. The hierarchy in the Trinity does not cease to exist at the ascension any more than the equality of Father and Son ceased to exist in the Incarnation. This is a paradox, but the early Church fathers believed that they must hold together both the eternal equality of the Trinity and the eternal hierarchy, since they could not allow the perception of any change in God over time. Thus, it is an eternal hierarchy, existing both before the Incarnation (seen in the divine visitations of the Old Testament) and after the ascension, and made manifest in the relationship of Father and Son as sender and messenger.

Therefore, this image of sitting at the right hand of the Father demonstrates both the unity and distinction of Father and Son. Since the Son is at the Father's right hand, he is unified with the Father's power and activity (inseparable operation). However, to be at the right hand also makes it clear that the Father and Son are not one and the same, since a person cannot be at his own right hand. This reminds us of John 1:1, where we read that the Word is both *God* (unity with the Father) and *with God* (distinction from the Father).

He will come again in glory
to judge the living and the dead

Some day, Jesus will return, but not in the human form of his Incarnation, and not circumscribed in one place only (Matthew 24:23–27). He will not come in humility as he once did, but he will come in glory. At this time, he will preside over the judgment of humanity. As the agent of the Father's judgment, the Son will continue his mission of exercising the Father's will with the Father's authority.

And his kingdom will have no end

This is a reference to the promise of an eternal kingdom in 2 Samuel, chapter 7. Since the political kingdom of David did not, in fact, last forever, this promise has been interpreted to mean that Jesus, a descendant of King David, will reign forever over a spiritual Kingdom. This is apparently how Jesus himself understood it (John 18:36). As Jesus taught in his parables, his Father is the king of the eternal kingdom, and he is the prince and heir (see Matthew, chapter 22). However, the sonship of Jesus and his unity with the Father make it appropriate also to call him the king, or "king of kings" (Revelation 17:14, 19:16).

I believe in the Holy Spirit, the Lord, the giver of life

The third major section of the Creed was expanded at the Council of Constantinople in 381 and affirms the divinity of the Holy Spirit. Just as the Father and the Son can both rightly be called "Lord," so can the Spirit (*CCC* 202). The fact that the Spirit is called "the giver of life" should not be taken in any modalistic sense (as if the Father and the Son are somehow not also givers of life), but here it specifically refers to the "breath of life" of creation (Genesis 2:7, keep in mind that the Hebrew word for "Spirit" can also mean "breath"). As we have seen, the

Holy Spirit was involved in the creation of the universe (Genesis 1:2). Just like the Father and the Son, the Holy Spirit is not created but is in fact Creator (*CCC* 291). Also like the Son, the Holy Spirit is not a receiver of life but giver of life. This makes it clear, in case there was any confusion, that the Holy Spirit of the New Testament is the same as the Spirit of God in the Old Testament. The Holy Spirit is equally divine with the Father and Son and equally Creator with the Father and Son.

The equality and divinity of the Holy Spirit can also be seen in passages that refer to the "blasphemy of the Holy Spirit," where Jesus makes it clear that an offense against the Spirit is an offense against God (Matthew 12:32, Mark 3:29, Luke 12:10, see also Acts 5:3, 7:51). The implication is that if the Spirit can be said to be a source of life, inspiration, sanctification, regeneration, and resurrection (John 3:5–8, Romans 8:11), then it must also be said that the Spirit is divine.

Who proceeds from the Father and the Son

Just as the Son is said to be begotten, or generated, from the Father, the Holy Spirit *proceeds* from the Father and the Son to the Church (John 15:26, 16:13–15) and to humanity. Although the concept of procession was used to describe the Son in early Christian texts, by the fourth century, procession became the specific personal term for the Spirit, to describe both the consubstantiality of the Spirit with the Father and the Son, but also to clarify the distinction of the Holy Spirit as a person of the Trinity.

The original version of the Creed (from the Council of Constantinople) only said that the Spirit proceeds from the Father. However, after the Councils of Nicaea and Constantinople, Arianism did not exactly go away. In fact, it moved west. In order to refute Arianism, some bishops in the western Church (including Saint Augustine) began emphasizing the equality of the Son with the Father by talking about the "double procession" of the Spirit—that the Spirit proceeds equally from the Father and the Son (John 14:26, 15:26, CCC 245–248). The western Church eventually added the phrase "and the Son," which in Latin is expressed by one word, *filioque*. Unfortunately, this change became a major factor in the split between eastern and western Christianity in 1054 and remains to this day the one difference in the creeds of the eastern and western churches.

Who with the Father and the Son is adored and glorified

Adoration is synonymous with worship. Just as is it appropriate to worship Jesus Christ, it is also appropriate to worship the Holy Spirit. We may sing songs to the Holy Spirit and pray to the Holy Spirit for the Spirit's presence and activity in our lives. Because of the one divine essence shared by the three persons of the Trinity, worshiping the Holy Spirit is worshiping God. We do not believe in three Gods, but we believe in one God who is manifest in three persons, and the Holy Spirit is as much a divine person as the Father and the Son. Therefore, the Spirit's full and equal divinity means that the Spirit may be worshiped without committing idolatry.

Who has spoken through the prophets

The Holy Spirit, who is both the Spirit of the Father and the Spirit of Christ (Romans 8:9, 1 Peter 1:11), is the same Spirit of the Lord who inspired the prophets of the Old Testament, as well as John the baptist. This further connects the Old and New Testaments, against those docetics and gnostics who would claim that the Creator of the Old Testament was not the same as the God of the New Testament. This line rounds out the third section of the Creed by affirming once again that God is one and what Christ did and said in his earthly ministry is consistent with God's overall plan of salvation, because he was inspired by the same Holy Spirit as the prophets.

At the same time, we cannot push this concept to the point of assigning inspiration to the Holy Spirit alone. The doctrine of inseparable operation reminds us that, technically speaking, it was the Trinity who inspired the prophets and apostles.

I believe in one, holy, catholic and apostolic Church

Although we have finished the Trinitarian three-point outline, there is a final section to the Creed. Actually, the Creed written by the bishops at Nicaea concluded with a series of condemnations for anyone who believed what the Arians taught. But at the Council of Constantinople, this was replaced with the section on the Church.

This line lists what are sometimes referred to as the four "marks" of the Church. We as Christians believe that Jesus Christ instituted the Church as the continuation of his own ministry (Matthew 16:18). The Church is *one*, in that it is meant to be unified in its teaching and its sacraments; it is *holy*, in that it was created by Christ and continued by his apostles to be the expression of God's presence in the world during the last age; it is *catholic*, in that it is universal, or worldwide; and it is *apostolic*, in that it is not only founded by the apostles, but it is also continuous with them—the contemporary Church is connected to the Church of the apostles through apostolic succession and the communion of the saints.

Unfortunately, the unity that Christ envisioned has suffered many schisms over the course of the history of the Church. Nevertheless, the Nicene Creed itself serves as one unifying factor, even across denominations that cannot share the sacraments.

I confess one baptism for the forgiveness of sins

The sacrament of baptism is common to almost all Christian denominations, and though it is done differently by some groups (for example sprinkling versus full immersion), most denominations will accept the baptism of another. Therefore baptism, as a sacrament of initiation, is one thing that should unify the body of Christ. As we have seen, this is not always the case, but it is the ideal envisioned by Christ and the apostles (John 17:20–21, Ephesians 4:5).

The fact that baptism is done "for the forgiveness of sins" means that it is not just a symbol or a ritual—it is a sacrament, with saving significance. The person being baptized receives God's grace (that is, God's love, mercy, and forgiveness), and that grace is effective for the recipient. When accepted in faith (by the one being baptized, or in the case of infants, by the parents and sponsors on behalf of the child), the one being baptized enters into the community of those whom God calls holy. However, as I have explained, a baptism must be done in the name of the Father, Son, and Holy Spirit in order to be valid (Matthew 28:18–20).

And I look forward to the resurrection of the dead and the life of the world to come. Amen.

The Creed ends with the hope of the Church. We believe that physical death is not the end of life and that those who follow Christ in life will follow him in resurrection after death. Of course, this is a mystery beyond our present understanding, but we are firm in our faith that there is life after death and that our identification with Christ promises us a share in his eternal inheritance.

As a summary of New Testament faith, the Creed gives us a handle on the difficult concept of the Trinity. Remember that though it is a paradox, it is really all about balance. The person of Christ is a perfect union of full divinity and full humanity. Within the Trinity, there is a harmony of equality and hierarchy. The three persons exist in a perfect balance of unity and distinction. The unity is found in the shared divinity, equal eternity, and unified divine activity of the Trinity. This divine unity, or consubstantiality, of the three persons of the Trinity means that, practically speaking, anything that can be said about one person of the Trinity can also be said about the other two persons, and anything that can be said about one person can also be said about the Trinity (and vice versa). This is the concept of appropriation. However, as I hinted above, there are a few exceptions to this rule. The distinction between the persons is found in those exceptions. The exceptions to the rule of appropriation are the few properties that are unique to one person of the Trinity. They are as follows:

The Father is <u>unbegotten</u> and is the ultimate Source of all existence. God the Father is Yahweh, the God of Abraham, Isaac, and Jacob in the Old Testament. He is the First Cause of all that exists. The fact that he is unbegotten (ungenerated) means that he is the *uncaused cause* of all that is. His existence is not derived from or dependent on the existence of any other being—not even the other two persons of the Trinity.

The Son is <u>begotten</u> and <u>incarnate</u>. God the Son is the preexistent Word (John 1:1–2) whom the world knows as the man Jesus of Nazareth, called the Christ. The fact that he is begotten (generated) means that his existence is derived from and dependent on the Father. However, the generation is eternal, meaning that the Son is co-eternal with the Father, and there was no time when the Son did not exist. The fact that he is incarnate means that he became human. Neither the Father nor the Spirit became human, however through inseparable operation, it must be assumed that all three persons of the Trinity were active in the Incarnation (Luke 1:31–32, 35). Note here the balance of unity and distinction in the Trinity: The Son is God, but the Son is not the Father, for if he were the Father, it could be said that the Father died on the cross (patripassionism), and God cannot die. Only the human nature of Christ experienced change, suffered, and died, not his divine nature. However, the unity of the divine and human natures means that both natures were circumscribed within the womb of Mary. In fact, the Incarnation is a manifestation of the circumscribability of the Son, which is not limited to the time of the Incarnation. Circumscribability is a personal property unique to the Son, which is also made manifest in the Old Testament theophanies of the "Angel of the Lord" and other pre-Incarnation appearances of the Divine.

The Holy Spirit _proceeds_ and indwells. The Holy Spirit is both the "Spirit of the Lord" of the Old Testament and the "Spirit of Christ" of the New Testament. The Spirit proceeds from the Father and the Son (double procession), but it is equally accurate to say that the Spirit proceeds from the Father _through_ the Son (the Son is the agent of procession). The fact that the Holy Spirit proceeds means that the Spirit is both consubstantial with the Father and the Son, as well as distinct from the Father and the Son. The Holy Spirit is the Spirit of Christ, but he is not one and the same as Christ, even in Christ's preexistent or post-ascension state. Just as the generation of the Son implies both the Son's consubstantiality with the Father and his distinction from the Father, the procession of the Spirit also implies both the Spirit's consubstantiality with, and distinction from, the Father and the Son. The Holy Spirit indwells believers, and even though both the Father and the Son are also omnipresent, the concept of indwelling is usually reserved specifically for the Holy Spirit.

These few attributes (unbegotten, begotten, incarnate, and proceeding) are the only things we can say are unique to one person of the Trinity. Anything else one can say about the persons of the Trinity (such as Creator, Savior, Sustainer) really apply to all three, and any attempt to distinguish the three persons by these modes of activity is a form of the heresy of modalism. In fact, the early Christian theologians like Tertullian would say that the distinction of persons exists within the unity, so that in a way the unity of the Trinity (the oneness of God) is primary. The three persons of the Trinity, though they are distinct, are not separate and are always oriented toward the unity. Even the activity of God *ad extra* (toward humanity) has as its goal to bring humanity back to the Trinity in reconciliation.

The concepts of divine simplicity, consubstantiality, and inseparable operation combine to describe God as a Trinity within which each divine person exists *in* the other two (John 14:10–11, *CCC* 255). This mutual interexistence of the three persons of the Trinity has several names. In Greek it is called *perichoresis*, or *emperichoresis*; in Latin, *circumincessio*; or in English, *reciprocity*. Whatever the name, the point is that in the Trinity, even the distinction between persons is at the service of the unity and is oriented toward the oneness of God. In a way, what *communicatio idiomatum* is to the two natures of Christ, *perichoresis* is to the persons of the Trinity—an overriding unity that nevertheless does not diminish the distinction. Some interpretations will trivialize the concept by saying that the word *perichoresis* means to "dance around," as if the three persons of the Trinity are dancing around some cosmic maypole of divine unity. However, the reality is much deeper than that, and it is precisely at this point that our human language breaks down and we must admit that we are at a loss to describe God in any complete way.

SUMMARY

We have seen the development of the Nicene Creed from the First Ecumenical Council of Nicaea (325 CE) through the Second Ecumenical Council of Constantinople (381). The Third Ecumenical Council of Ephesus (431) and the Fourth Ecumenical Council of Chalcedon (451) expanded on the Church's understanding of christology, but they did not write a new Creed. Each affirmed the Creed of Nicaea-Constantinople and added some clarifications. The Chalcedonian definition further clarified the relationship of divinity and humanity in the person of Christ. In describing the Church's understanding of the two natures, neither nature can be diminished or said to have changed, and the union of natures cannot imply the creation of some third thing that would seem to obscure the full divinity of the divine nature or the full humanity of the human nature. Thus the balance of unity and distinction that we see in the persons of the Trinity is also extended to the two natures within the person of Christ. The two natures are one, but not the same; distinct, but not separate.

We began with the problem of Christian monotheism. How can we call ourselves monotheists if we worship Jesus? The answer is a balance, which can be described as a middle way between extreme alternatives—a position that refuses to deny any part of the biblical witness about Christ in spite of the fact that the result may seem like a paradox (1 Corinthians 1:23). Is Christ human or divine? Both. Is God one or three? Both. Does the Trinity exhibit equality or hierarchy? Both. Is salvation a matter of divine intervention or human representation? It's both (with the priority on divine intervention as God's initiative). Is the Christian life a matter of personal devotion or works of charity? It's both. Is the kingdom of God here now or coming later? Yes, both. The concept of the "Word made flesh" was seen as an impossibility by many people in the ancient world. And yet, with the guidance of the triune God, the Church came to the conclusion that even though it is a paradox, it is nevertheless true.

To conclude this chapter, the first four ecumenical councils can be summarized as follows:

The Council of Nicaea (325)

Confronted Arius (who diminished the divinity of Christ)

Affirmed that "begotten" does not mean created

Affirmed the christology of descent against Arius' christology of ascent

Concluded that the Son is consubstantial with the Father:

The full divinity of the Son (same divinity)

The Son is co-eternal with the Father (same eternity)

The Council of Constantinople (381)

Confronted Pneumatomachians (who denied the divinity of the Spirit)

Confronted Apollinarius (who diminished the humanity of Christ)

Affirmed the full humanity of the Son (not just flesh, but human)

Affirmed the full divinity of the Spirit

Expanded the Creed of Nicaea

The Council of Ephesus (431)

Reaffirmed the condemnation of Apollinarius

Confronted Nestorius (who diminished the union of natures in Christ)

Concluded that it is appropriate to call Mary, "Mother of God"

The Council of Chalcedon (451)

Reaffirmed the condemnation of Nestorius

Confronted Eutyches (who diminished the humanity of Christ)

The Chalcedonian Definition
    In the two natures of Christ, a balance of unity and distinction
    In three persons of the Trinity, a balance of unity and distinction

DISCUSSION QUESTIONS

1. What was the orthodox counter-slogan to Arius' "there was a time when he was not," and what does it mean for the understanding of God as a Trinity?

2. Why does our salvation depend on the "christology of descent"?

3. Why is it important that our creed clarifies that the God whom Jesus called "Father" is also the Creator?

4. What does it mean that the Son is begotten (generated), while the Father is unbegotten (ungenerated)?

5. What does it mean that the Father and the Son (and the Spirit) are consubstantial? Can you explain consubstantiality to someone using the shortcut of two simple concepts?

6. What is the doctrine of "divine simplicity"? How is it related to divine immutability, divine impassibility, and divine incorruptibility?

7. Why is Mary's title "Mother of God" appropriate, and what does this title teach us about Jesus Christ?

8. How does our creed affirm the divinity of the Holy Spirit?

9. What does it mean that the Holy Spirit proceeds, and why is this a source of tension between Western and Eastern Christians?

10. What is the "doctrine of appropriation," and what are the few exceptions to the rule?

CHAPTER 4

Analogies for the Trinity

It's been said that more heresy is (accidentally) preached on Trinity Sunday than at any other time of the year. This is because, as we have seen, the doctrine of the Trinity is difficult to understand and it is even more difficult to explain. When we have to explain the doctrine of the Trinity, we often resort to analogies of "three in one." This may be the best option we have, though all analogies ultimately fall short because none of them completely captures the balance between oneness (unity) and "threeness" (distinction). They are all either too heavy on the unity with not enough distinction (and thus become more of an analogy for modalism) or they are too heavy on the distinction with not enough unity (describing a version of adoptionism/Arianism rather than orthodoxy). There is a Latin saying regarding the Trinity that goes, *Opera trinitatis ad extra sunt indivisa, servato discrimine et ordine personarum*. Translated into English it means, "The external works of the Trinity are indivisible, (yet) the distinction and order of persons are preserved."

It is this balance of unity (singular essence and indivisible activity) and distinction (eternal distinction/hierarchy of persons, but not described in terms of function) that we strive for in explaining the Trinity with analogies—but which proves to be elusive. The problem is that no analogy from the created world can successfully exemplify both the oneness and the threeness all at the same time. A thing is either one thing with three parts, or three things that have some common relationship, but nothing that we can observe is truly always both one and three at the same time. We're trying to use creation to describe the Creator, and since creation is finite, that only gets us so far. Nevertheless, it will be helpful to take a look at a few analogies for the Trinity. There are three kinds of analogies for the Trinity (appropriate, isn't it?). They are: natural analogies, personal analogies, and social analogies.

NATURAL ANALOGIES: *VESTIGIA TRINITATIS IN CREATURA*

The Latin phrase means "traces of the Trinity in creation," which is what we mean by a natural analogy. There are things we can observe in the universe around us that hint at a triune Creator. For example, there are three primary colors and all the colors combine to make white light. There are three primary musical notes in a chord and three primary chords in any composition. Also, the ancients understood the human person to have three parts (body, soul, and spirit/mind, see Hebrews 4:12). Therefore there are many images in nature that have been used to describe the Trinity.

Saint Patrick is said to have used a clover to illustrate how God is three in one. The clover is one flower with one stem yet with three leaves. This analogy does begin to create a picture of "three in one," yet it doesn't quite have the balance of unity and distinction that we're looking for. Specifically, the unity is compromised by the perception that the three leaves are parts of the one flower—parts which could be plucked off the stem. Remember that the Trinity cannot be described as having parts that can be separated. What is more, if one of the leaves were to be separated from the stem, it would not contain the fullness of the clover by itself. However, in the Trinity, each person of the Trinity is fully divine.

Another illustration from nature that is often used to describe the Trinity is an egg. The egg has three components:

shell, white, and yolk. (The analogy of an apple is basically the same, with three components of skin, flesh, and core). Again, this analogy falls short because none of the three components by itself contains the full essence of the egg. Within the Trinity, however, each person of the Trinity has full divinity in and of himself. Though it is a shared divinity, it is not the case that the Son of God, for example, has only one third of the divinity (Colossians 2:9). These analogies from nature would imply a God who has "parts" which could be separated (neglecting the concept of divine simplicity), and which do not contain the fullness of the whole in and of themselves.

Water is another often-used analogy. Water (H_2O) can exist as a solid (ice), a liquid (water), or a gas (steam). The problem with this analogy is that while water can exist in these three forms, it can only be in one form at a time. It cannot be all three at the same time. Therefore, this analogy actually describes more of a modalistic view of the Trinity, since in modalism God is described by three names but can only be one at a time (the Father in the Old Testament, the Son in the New Testament, and the Spirit in the Church).

One of the better analogies from nature is that of the sun. The early theologians used this analogy (but so did some of the heretics). The sun is a star, which emits both light and heat. Together the star, the light, and the heat make up the one sun. The unity of the sun is in the indivisible operation of the three elements. In other words, all three are unified in their activity, and it is virtually impossible to tell where one ends and another begins. The distinction between the three is found in the fact that each has a particular relationship to the other two, with the star itself as the Source of the light and heat. Furthermore, both the light and the heat are dependent on the star for their existence, and yet there was no time when the star existed without the light and heat. And if we want to push the analogy a step further, we can say that if the sun represents the triune God, we can be the moon, reflecting the light of God into otherwise darkened places. This is not a perfect analogy, because like the egg or the apple, the three parts cannot be said to have the essence of the whole in and of themselves. Still, this is one of the best of the natural analogies, and it has the advantage of avoiding a modalistic interpretation because all three (star, light, and heat) exist at the same time.

Finally, what might be the best analogy from nature is that of the universe itself. While this one is a bit obscure, the point is that it is a *uni*-verse, one realm that exists in three dimensions. The oneness is in the singularity of the universe, the "threeness" is in its three-dimensional nature.

PERSONAL ANALOGIES

Personal analogies are those in which one person is described in three different ways. The unity is in the fact that it is a single person, the distinction is in the three ways that the person is perceived. The flaw in all personal analogies is that since it is only one person, there will never be enough distinction between the three perceptions of that person to demonstrate the balance of unity and distinction in the Trinity.

For example, a man can be a father to one person, a son to another, and a brother to yet another. In this way, the man is sometimes said to be an image of the Trinity because he is one man, perceived in three different ways. The biggest problem with this analogy is that the man cannot be all three (father and son and brother) to the same person, so that (like the analogy of water) the "threeness" of this analogy can be only one at a time and therefore this is a picture of a modalistic understanding of God. What is more, the distinction is not real but is a perceived distinction only relative to the observer, which is another characteristic of modalism.

The human psyche is another analogy that is sometimes used for the Trinity. In this analogy, the id, ego, and super-ego are the three manifestations of the one psyche. However, as with all personal analogies, there does not seem to be enough distinction in the balance, because, after all, it is only one person. A variation of this analogy that has been used is one person with multiple personalities. This is an attempt to bring more distinction into the balance by assuming three distinct personalities within one person. The problem with this is that multiple personality disorder is just that—a *disorder* in the human psyche—and multiple personalities are often either ignorant of or hostile toward each other. Also, it seems one would need a better-than-average understanding of psychology to understand or explain analogies based on the human psyche.

Saint Augustine experimented with a few personal analogies, though he admitted that they all had their limitations. He used an analogy similar to that of the human psyche, in which the intellect, memory, and will represented the three persons of the Trinity. This is actually a combination of a personal analogy and an analogy from nature (the three-part human being). The danger of this analogy is that if we think of the three aspects of the person as three activities (thinking, remembering, and willing), then it could become modalistic. Thomas Aquinas would later develop this analogy and realize its potential for a description of the Trinity as distinction within unity.

The best of the personal analogies is probably that of human speech. Speech has been used to describe the Trinity, in that it is comprised of an idea (in the mind of the speaker), the words used (that is, the linguistic terms that contain the idea and have meaning for the listener), and the breath or sound waves that carry the words to the audience. This analogy does have the advantage of demonstrating the unity of activity within the Trinity quite well. It also has a convenient play on words, in which the *words* in the analogy represent Jesus Christ, the Word of God, and the *breath* represents the Holy Spirit, the Breath of Life (*CCC* 689).

SOCIAL ANALOGIES

Social analogies are, in a way, the opposite of personal analogies. Rather than one person with three parts, a social analogy imagines three people who have something in common. The distinction is in the fact that there are three different people, and the unity is in their relationship—whatever it is they have in common. There is plenty of distinction in this kind of analogy, but these are often lacking in unity. There is not enough unity because the analogy assumes three completely separate people. Therefore, while some of the analogies above run the risk of modalism, social analogies run the risk of adoptionism.

One example of a social analogy is identical triplets: one set of DNA, with three distinct personalities. This one gets close, however there is still not enough unity, since even triplets are not necessarily unified in any permanent sense. They may come from a single source, but there is no ongoing tie binding them together in the present and future. In other words, there is nothing inherent in them preventing them from moving to different cities and never speaking to each other again. Though they have a unified origin, they are more than distinct, they are separate, and therefore this analogy does not have enough unity.

Saint Augustine used the idea of a loving relationship as an analogy, in which the Father is described as the lover, the Son as the beloved, and the Holy Spirit as the love that unites them. However, this analogy is problematic because it might give the impression that the Spirit is an impersonal attribute of God or that the Spirit is to be equated with the substance of divinity. In either case, the analogy risks making the Holy Spirit seem impersonal, more like a "thing," than a divine person. Incidentally, we should avoid referring to the Holy Spirit with the pronoun, "it" for the same reason.

The best social analogy is that of the family (*CCC* 2205). While we acknowledge that families come in all types and configurations, imagine a family of three: a father, mother and one child. If the oneness of the family can be symbolized in the family home, we do get something like Tertullian's concept that the distinction is within the unity. If we assume that the child represents the Holy Spirit, we could say (like the western Creed) that the child "proceeds" from the father and the mother. However, this analogy still lacks unity, because they are three different people and certainly at least the child will one day go off on his own. Also, we must avoid giving the impression that the Father has (or needs) a divine spouse. To put it another way, we must never give the impression that (for example) the Father and the Spirit are somehow the divine "parents" of the Son, since this would imply a kind of cosmic coupling or procreation such as one finds in paganism and gnosticism. Still, of all the social analogies, this one comes closest to being a good representation of the Trinity.

Sometimes it is stated that the Trinity can be used as an analogy for human relationships. In other words, some claim that we should look to the Trinity as a model for human community. There may be some merit to this, however it runs the risk of creating God in our own image. In other words, just as the social analogies for the Trinity are ultimately inadequate, trying to use the Trinity (who is beyond human experience) to describe human relationships will also be inadequate because it fails to do justice to the transcendence of God.

Therefore, if one is tempted to try to explain the Trinity using analogies, one must be careful to maintain the balance of unity and distinction, or oneness and "threeness," that the early theologians worked so hard to define. So if one uses natural or personal analogies, one must be careful to avoid modalism by making it clear that the three persons of the Trinity exist as all three always (all at the same time). If one uses social analogies, one must be careful to avoid adoptionism by emphasizing that all three persons of the Trinity are unified in all activity and that Jesus Christ is both fully human and fully divine. In the end, the reality that early heretics used some of the same analogies as the orthodox theologians shows that it is not really the analogy itself, so much as the explanation of the analogy that teaches something about the Trinity. No analogy on its own will ever be adequate—it is only in the use of that analogy for catechesis that it may become helpful for understanding the Trinity.

One must also keep in mind that children are not yet able to do abstract reasoning, and therefore it is very difficult for anyone under the age of about twelve or thirteen to understand any analogies, let alone those which try to describe the Trinity. When it comes to teaching children, it is advisable to stay away from analogies and metaphors and stick with the few things they will need to participate in liturgy, such as saying the Creed and crossing themselves. They can be promised that they will grow in understanding as they get older.

Finally, when analogies fail, the only option left may be to describe the Trinity by saying what the Trinity is not. The Trinity is not three gods. The Trinity is also not simply three masks, or hats, worn by the one God when he wants to perform different functions.

ANSWERS TO COMMON UNITARIAN OBJECTIONS

Unitarians are the modern legacy of the Adoptionists and Arians, and include Unitarian Universalists, members of "Oneness" movements, and Jehovah's Witnesses. Like the early Adoptionists, they do not accept the doctrine of the Trinity, justifying this by saying that they are defending the oneness of God. And like the Arians and Pneumatomachians of the fourth century, they often accuse us of worshiping three Gods. In short, they are Unitarian because they are not Trinitarian.

The primary objection of the Unitarians is that the word "Trinity" is not found in the Bible. As we have seen, this was also an objection of the Arians (regarding the word homoousios, or consubstantial). However, it is a false premise that orthodox theology can only use terms found in Scripture, since all expressions of Judeo-Christian faith make use of important terms not found in Scripture and which become essential to the interpretation of Scripture. The concept of sola scriptura, when taken to an extreme, would leave one with no tradition—and it is in the tradition that we find the Church's interpretation of Scripture.

Some Unitarians will also argue that the doctrine of the Trinity was a product of the Council of Nicaea and did not exist before the fourth century. Some even give the credit to the emperor Constantine, claiming that he was one who invented the doctrine of the Trinity. However, as we have seen, that is not the case. Even if the doctrine of the Trinity is not spelled out in Scripture, the concepts on which it is built are evident in Scripture, and it is clear that the apostles and early Church fathers understood God as a Trinity. By the mid-third century, Tertullian had defined consubstantiality and Novatian had described eternal generation.

Therefore, as we have seen, the doctrine of the Trinity was not a later development, but emerged from the teachings of the apostles and the interpretation of Scripture, precisely as a way to describe why the worship of Christ was not a form of idolatry and why those who worship Christ could still be called monotheists.

What to Say When Jehovah's Witnesses Come to Your Door

You may have had the experience of Jehovah's Witnesses coming to your home and inviting you to consider their beliefs. Although they may tell you that they believe in Jesus Christ, they are not Christians as defined by the Nicene Creed. The Jehovah's Witnesses believe that Jesus was a man who became a god. This is clear in their translation of John 1:1. Where the Gospel of John says, "In the beginning was the Word, and the Word was with God, and the Word was God," the Jehovah's Witnesses' *New World Translation* says, "In the beginning was the Word, and the Word was with God, and the Word was *a god*." This is the Arian christology of ascent, which says that God is one because Jesus Christ was not originally divine by nature, but he was a mere man who became a god (a lesser divinity).

When the Jehovah's Witnesses come to your door, there is probably nothing you can say that they have not heard. Even though their translation of John 1:1 is incorrect, you would not be able to convince them of that. Plus, chances are good that the person at your door is only someone who has memorized the answers to a variety of questions, hoping that you won't have deeper questions for their answers. If you do ask deeper questions, they will simply call their "supervisor" and you will find yourself having the same conversation all over again. The best thing to say is that you are a Trinitarian Christian, and you're happy with that. They will understand that you know what you're talking about and that you won't be swayed by their arguments. If they press the issue, explain that you understand the theology behind the question and that you believe that Jesus Christ is the divine Son of God, equal in eternity and divinity (consubstantial) with the Father. Tell them that in our Creed we profess that the Holy Spirit proceeds from the Father and the Son, and that is your belief. At this point, they should move on to your next-door neighbors. If, however, you do find yourself engaged in a conversation about theology, you might get the opportunity to use one of the analogies above to explain your Trinitarian beliefs to your new Unitarian/Arian friend.

CONCLUSION

The doctrine of the Trinity is the product of both Scripture and tradition—Scripture as revelation, tradition as interpretation—but both are inspired by God. In fact, the process of the development of doctrine was itself inspired by God. And while we may be used to saying that this inspiration is a work of the Holy Spirit, the doctrine of inseparable operation reminds us that it is actually the Trinity (and not only one particular person of the Trinity) who inspired the words of the prophets, the writings of the apostles, and the interpretations of the Church fathers. This should prevent us from describing the three persons of the Trinity by functional, or modalistic, labels. Inseparable operation further requires that whatever we might say about one person of the Trinity can be said of the other persons, and vice versa, with a few exceptions. These exceptions (the Father is unbegotten, the Son is begotten and incarnate, and the Holy Spirit proceeds) provide the only real distinction between the three persons.

The fact that the incarnate one was also the risen one led to the conviction that we should worship Jesus Christ, which in turn compelled the early Church to redefine monotheism to include the person of Christ in the Divine. In its discernment of biblical truth and its description of what was determined to be correct interpretations of Scripture (orthodoxy), the theologians of the early Church defined the doctrine of the Trinity as an understanding of God that contains both unity and distinction. The unity, or oneness, of God was required to maintain monotheism, but the distinction was also required to maintain the immutability of the Divine.

We have observed "Papandrea's three laws" of the development of doctrine. After an initial phase in which Christian liturgy (the worship of Christ) begged the question, it would become clear that the presence of alternative interpretations would force the Church to clarify its definition of orthodoxy (law 1: *heresy forces orthodoxy to define itself*).

Thus the unity of the triune God was affirmed against both adoptionism and the various forms of polytheism, including gnosticism. The distinction of persons in the Trinity was affirmed against modalism. As Novatian had said, the orthodox Christ was being crucified again between the two thieves of adoptionism and modalism (law 2: *orthodoxy is the middle way between the extreme alternatives*).

Some of these alternatives were considered incorrect interpretations because they denied or diminished the real humanity of Christ, thus compromising humanity's connection to the Divine through him. Some were considered incorrect because they denied or diminished the divinity of Christ, thus compromising his connection to God, which again would threaten our reconciliation with God in salvation. Therefore, each interpretation of Christ and his relationship to the Father has implications for salvation (law 3: *christology informs soteriology*).

Thus we see that the loss of either Christ's full divinity or his real humanity, or for that matter the loss of the balance of unity and distinction in the Trinity, would seem to threaten humanity's hope for reconciliation with God. Too much distinction and not enough unity between the Father and the Son results in the loss or diminishing of Jesus' divinity, which implies a salvation by human effort. Too much unity without enough distinction in the Trinity results in the loss or diminishing of Jesus' humanity, which implies a salvation by enlightenment, or one that includes no real human representation or participation. The heresies were considered unacceptable because they each led to a soteriology that, the bishops determined, would not save. Arianism's christology of ascent will not raise humanity up. Only the christology of descent, in which God comes to be one of us in the Incarnation, has the ability to redeem humanity.

Christ is consubstantial with the Trinity in his divine nature and consubstantial with humanity in his human nature. We remain in him through the indwelling of the Holy Spirit, and by participation in the sacraments. Therefore, by virtue of the union of divine and human in the person of Christ, we are united with God. Also, the indwelling of the Spirit keeps us connected to all members of the body of Christ (past, present, and future) in the communion of the saints (*CCC* 1108).

Finally, when it comes to describing our understanding of the Trinity, we have to be careful not to assume that an analogy alone will suffice. As I have noted, it is really the explanation of any analogy that carries meaning. Remember that Tertullian gave us the terminology to speak of the Trinity as three "persons" (Latin: *personae*) sharing one substance (Latin: *substantia*). That substance is divinity itself. The word "persons" is a technical term for the three members of the Trinity. God is not three "people" (that would imply too much distinction and not enough unity), God is three persons (and not three parts). The point is that it is important to choose our words carefully. Sometimes heresy is taught by accident because people are not careful with language. In the end, words can only take us to far, because words are part of creation and God is the Creator. The concept of circumscription applies even to the understanding of the Trinity, since if we could fully understand the Trinity, that would be a kind of mental circumscription. The Trinity cannot be circumscribed—not even by our words or our thoughts—because God is a mystery. But it helps to begin to understand that mystery if we think of God in terms of perfect balance:

- ✍ The Trinity is a perfect balance of oneness and threeness.

- ✍ The Trinity is a perfect balance of unity and distinction of persons.

- ✍ The second person of the Trinity is a perfect balance of true humanity and full divinity.

- ✍ The second person of the Trinity is a perfect balance of the union and distinction of the two natures.

- ✍ Orthodox belief is the middle way between the extreme interpretations.

In spite of the challenge, clergy and laity alike should know how to explain this central aspect of our faith, in the spirit of 1 Peter 3:15, "Always be ready to give an explanation to anyone who asks you for a reason for your hope."

DISCUSSION QUESTIONS

1. Why is it that all analogies for the Trinity fall short of adequately describing God?

2. What are the three kinds of analogies for the Trinity?

3. What is the problem with using H2O as an analogy for the Trinity?

4. What is your favorite natural analogy—how does it describe the Trinity well, and in what way(s) does it fall short? Remember that any analogy is only as good as its explanation!

5. What is the inherent flaw in all personal analogies for the Trinity?

6. What is your favorite personal analogy—how does it describe the Trinity well, and in what way(s) does it fall short?

7. What is the inherent flaw in all social analogies for the Trinity?

8. What is your favorite social analogy—how does it describe the Trinity well, and in what way(s) does it fall short?

9. Why is it futile to try to use analogies to explain the Trinity to children?

10. Why does our hope of reconciliation with God and salvation depend on the two natures of Jesus Christ (true divinity and true humanity) and the doctrine of the Trinity?

Devotion to the Trinity

'd like to end with a word on the Trinity and personal devotion. When it comes to prayer and devotion to God, it is important to remember that God has created us so that there are no two people alike. What this means is that there are no two relationships with God that are the same (*CCC* 2672). God gave you a unique personality, and that personality determines your personal devotional style and how you will relate to God. God wants you to have a personal relationship with him, but God does not expect that your relationship with him needs to be exactly like anyone else's.

If you are interested in exploring this concept further, I highly recommend the book *Prayer and Temperament* by Chester P. Michael. In this book, Monsignor Michael discusses the relationship between personality type and devotional style. One of the conclusions of the book is that some people will naturally gravitate toward God as Father, others will relate better to God as Son (Jesus), and still others will be more attracted to the Holy Spirit. There is nothing wrong with this, because as we have seen, worshiping one person of the Trinity is as good as worshiping all three, and to worship any one person of the Trinity IS worshiping God. Therefore, it's OK if you have a favorite, or if you switch back and forth, because the unity of the divine Trinity guarantees that you are not neglecting the Father and the Spirit if (for example) you focus on the Son. And when you conclude your prayer, if you cross yourself in the name of the Father, Son, and Holy Spirit, you are affirming your belief in the Trinity. So I hope you will explore your newly expanded understanding of the Trinity in your prayer life. To get you started, I will conclude by offering a few prayers to the Holy Trinity.

Peace,

JIM L. PAPANDREA, PHD
jimpapandrea.com

Prayer to the Father

Our Heavenly Father,
May you be honored in all the world.
May your kingdom be revealed to the world.
May we do your will in the world.
Thank you for the way you provide for us every day.
I am sorry for my sins and pray that you will overlook them.
Help me to overlook the faults of my friends and enemies.
Protect me from evil, from danger, and, if necessary,
from myself. Amen.

(Adapted from the Our Father by Jim Papandrea.
See the author's *Pray, Not Just Say, the Lord's Prayer.*)

Prayer to the Son

Lord Jesus, you are worthy to reveal the will of God and
enforce it
Because you gave your life to save people of every race and
nation for God.
And you have made them into a new people of ambassadors
for God,
And they will share in your victory and in your Kingdom.

The Lamb of God who was crucified is now glorified.
You are worthy of all power and authority and lordship,
And all wisdom and honor and praise and blessing.
Blessing and honor and glory and sovereignty
Belong to God the Father and to the Lamb of God forever.

Your works are great and wonderful,
Oh Lord, all-powerful God.
Your ways are true and righteous,
Oh King of all the nations.

Who would dare not glorify you, Oh Lord?
For you alone are holy.
People of every nation will worship you in your presence
Because your justice has been revealed.
Salvation comes from God and from the Lamb! Amen.

(Adapted from the Book of Revelation by Jim Papandrea.
See the author's *Wedding of the Lamb.*)

Prayer to the Holy Spirit

Oh fire of the Helping Spirit,
the life of every creature's life,
you are holy in giving life to forms.
You are holy in anointing the severely injured,
holy in cleansing foul wounds.
Oh breath of holiness, fire of love,
oh sweet taste in our bodies
and pouring in our hearts of the fragrance of all virtues.
Oh clearest fountain,
in which is shown how God gathers together
those who wander and seeks those who are lost...
Let there be praise to you
who are the sound of all praise and the joy of life,
who are hope and powerful honor,
granting the gifts of light. Amen.

(Saint Hildegard of Bingen, twelfth century.
See the author's *Rome: A Pilgrim's Guide to the Eternal City.*)

Prayer to the Holy Trinity

Almighty, eternal, just and merciful God,
grant us in our misery the grace to do for you alone
what we know you want us to do,
and always to desire what pleases you.
Thus, inwardly cleansed, inwardly enlightened,
and inflamed by the fire of the Holy Spirit,
may we be able to follow in the footprints of your beloved Son,
our Lord Jesus Christ.
And by your grace alone, may we make our way to you,
Most High, who live and rule in perfect Trinity and
simple Unity
and are glorified,
God all-powerful, forever and ever. Amen.

(Saint Francis of Assisi, thirteenth century.
See the author's *Rome: A Pilgrim's Guide to the Eternal City*.)

Recommended Readings for Further Study

Jesus 101, by John L. Gresham

Holy Spirit 101, by John L. Gresham

Lord Jesus Christ: Devotion to Jesus in Earliest Christianity, by Larry Hurtado

The Real Jesus, by Luke Timothy Johnson

Prayer and Temperament, by Chester P. Michael and Marie C. Norrisey

Rome: A Pilgrim's Guide to the Eternal City, by James Papandrea

Novatian of Rome and the Culmination of Pre-Nicene Orthodoxy,
    by James Papandrea

Reading the Early Church Fathers, by James Papandrea

The Wedding of the Lamb: A Historical Approach to the Book of Revelation,
    by James Papandrea

Spiritual Blueprint: How We Live, Work, Love, Play and Pray,
    by James Papandrea

Pray (Not Just Say) the Lord's Prayer, by James Papandrea

How to Be a Saint, by James Papandrea

The Humanity of Jesus in the Fourth Gospel, by Marianne Meye Thompson

CPSIA information can be obtained
at www.ICGtesting.com
Printed in the USA
LVHW02s2115130318
569690LV00003B/6/P

9 780764 820823